D0437361

THE SPIRITUAL LEGACY *of*
LAURA INGALLS WILDER

A Prairie Girl's Faith

STEPHEN W. HINES

WATERBROOK

A Prairie Girl's Faith

All Scripture quotations, unless otherwise indicated, are taken from the King James Version. Scripture quotations marked (NASB) are taken from the New American Standard Bible®. Copyright © 1960, 1962, 1963, 1968, 1971, 1972, 1973, 1975, 1977, 1995 by the Lockman Foundation. Used by permission. (www.Lockman.org). Scripture quotations marked (NIV) are taken from the Holy Bible, New International Version®, NIV®. Copyright © 1973, 1978, 1984 by Biblica Inc.® Used by permission. All rights reserved worldwide.

Pioneer Girl text © 2014 Little House Heritage Trust and South Dakota Historical Society Press. All rights reserved. Used by permission.

Permission to quote from *The De Smet News* was granted by Dale Blegen, publisher.

Hardcover ISBN 978-0-7352-8978-9
eBook ISBN 978-0-7352-8979-6

Copyright © 2018 by Stephen W. Hines

Cover design by Kristopher K. Orr; cover painting by William Affleck, Bridgeman Images

Published in the United States by WaterBrook, an imprint of the Crown Publishing Group, a division of Penguin Random House LLC, New York.

WATERBROOK® and its deer colophon are registered trademarks of Penguin Random House LLC.

The Cataloging-in-Publication Data is on file with the Library of Congress.

Printed in the United States of America
2018—First Edition

10 9 8 7 6 5 4 3 2 1

SPECIAL SALES
Most WaterBrook books are available at special quantity discounts when purchased in bulk by corporations, organizations, and special-interest groups. Custom imprinting or excerpting can also be done to fit special needs. For information, please e-mail specialmarketscms@penguinrandom house.com or call 1-800-603-7051.

For Gwen—who else?

Contents

Introduction

As a child I learned my Bible lessons by heart, in the
good old-fashioned way, and once won the prize for
repeating correctly . . . verses from the Bible.

—LAURA INGALLS WILDER

y the fourth grade at Victory Elementary School in Miami
County, Kansas, I was mostly literate but had run out of
reading material. I was tired of *Silver Chief: Dog of the North, White
Fang,* and *My Friend Flicka.* The youth culture of my age was fixated
either on Lassie or on young teens living impossible adventures, like the
Hardy Boys. I couldn't identify with these characters.

Down the road from our old two-room schoolhouse, which bulged
with a student population of fifty-two, I could see the older one-room
schoolhouse, made of stone to last forever, that was now a hay shed. The
hay it held was probably a grass that is known as little bluestem. We
called it buffalo grass, and I'm sure the buffalo did eat it when they
roamed the prairie. Up and down both sides of the road that led to
school were stone walls behind which "tall" buffalo grass grew and
further completed a very rustic picture of our school environment. We

thought we were children of the plains and were inspired by some books from Bobbs-Merrill Publishing Company titled Childhood of Famous Americans, a series that assured us we came from excellent heritage and sterling stock.

Is it any wonder then that I should pick up a book off our thinly stocked library shelves, one I hadn't noticed before with an illustration of a young girl skipping across the top of an old dugout house covered with grass and snuggled into a bank by a stream?

On the Banks of Plum Creek was my own little secret discovery. It looked like a girls' book, so I probably didn't display it much when I became absorbed in its pages. But it was unlike any book I'd read up until then. Laura Ingalls was telling her story from her personal point of view, and every family member seemed as real as the people I knew around me. We didn't have any sod shanties about, but we sure had a lot of rugged-looking land! That is why the tone of Laura's personal narrative made me warm to her immediately.

Geography was not one of my better subjects in school, so when I first came across the book *On the Banks of Plum Creek,* I associated the title with the creek that ran only a quarter mile from our church. This thinking seemed natural to me: Plum Creek Methodist Church was where I attended, and, of course, Laura must have settled nearby. Why, I knew she had lived in Kansas at one time, so my conclusion seemed logical for a fourth grader! It didn't take me long to figure out the error of my ways, but that feeling of kinship with Laura had only grown.

Most of all, what drew me further into the world of Laura and her family was that the more I read of her pioneer life, the more I felt I had met a kindred spirit who, if we ever met, I would know at once as a friend. Laura and I were imaginary playmates, after a fashion. Why, we even shared some Methodist experiences and probably sang some of the same hymns.

I am a descendant of pioneers myself. The first Hines—so far as I have been able to determine by the records my father gathered—takes us back to the American Revolution and to somewhere in the East, maybe Virginia, but no farther. I have to settle for that. We can't all have come over on the *Mayflower*.

George Washington Hines (or perhaps Hinds) sired four sons who served in the Civil War. At least I have a note to that effect in the family archives. One of his sons, Henry, born in 1846, lived to be ninety-two and died in 1938, well after my own father had been born. My dad served in the Marine Corps during World War II and right after that got married and began farming in eastern Kansas.

Although it was after World War II, Victor W. Hines was also a pioneer. Dad bought forty acres and our house for about $2,000 back in 1948. We moved into that place with no plumbing, no electricity, and no furnace. It was a cold frame building, heated by wood, and in some spots in the wall you could see right through to the outside. After all these years that still seems sort of like pioneering to me and is why I take up the story and values of Laura Ingalls Wilder's Little House series so earnestly.

Knowing more about Laura's homesteading experiences has become a lifelong pursuit, and my conviction has grown that her Christian pilgrimage is important to us all. Pioneer values of hope, endurance, courage, and religious conviction, shaped by our Lord and his teaching, have given us a vision of America that we should strive for. Some recent books have tended to dismiss the past as presented to us by Mrs. Wilder, but I myself cannot feel this way. Our forebears were not perfect examples of what Christians should look like; nevertheless, this woman and her beloved family give us a picture of a healthy, loving faith. And they can guide us all into the future as we grow in our faith.

Let us begin Laura's journey, which is our journey as well.

Pioneer Faith

There is no turning back nor standing still; we must
go forward, into the future, generation after generation
toward the accomplishment of the ends that have been
set for the human race.

—LAURA INGALLS WILDER

Virtually every reader and fan of Laura Ingalls Wilder's children's books comes to realize that her religious faith is woven into her family's story of pioneering in the old West. Throughout the eight original titles there are, in the foreground, references to Scripture, hymns, and prayer—to a daily life that experienced the reality of God.

We are no more than twenty-three pages into the first title, *Little House in the Big Woods,* before Pa is playing his fiddle from which poured such standards as "Rock of Ages," "On Jordan's Stormy Banks I Stand," and "A Shelter in the Time of Storm," songs that were in the hymnals of my youth but are seldom found sixty years later.

To find the roots of Laura's faith, we must, of course, discover

what we can about the spiritual journey of her parents, Charles and
Caroline.

The Family That Travels Together Stays Together

Fortunately, Dr. John E. Miller, professor emeritus of history at South
Dakota State University, has noted their journey and gives us some insights into early Ingalls and Quiner (Ma Ingalls) beginnings. Any re-
counting would be almost a blank without his work, but even he cannot
tell us everything. (For example, we know that Ma's father drowned in
Lake Michigan when Ma was only four, but we do not really know the
overall effect this had on her.)

What Miller does tell us is that both the Ingalls and Quiner families, along with many other families of their day, saw almost all their
hopes for economic gain to be in traveling west. There needed to be a
movement from the crowded East into the vastness of the "wilderness."
Their faith and family backgrounds certainly went with them on the
journey.

Grandma and Grandpa Ingalls (Laura and Lansford) migrated all
the way from Cuba, New York, to the woods of Wisconsin. Both of
them would have grown up in a sort of mixed Puritan and Congregational background common to the times. They would have considered
themselves in the mainstream of Protestantism of that day, with elements of reformational teaching of the Bible as an absolute authority on
doctrine, supplemented by attitudes that came out of the Great Awakening led by Jonathan Edwards (1703–58).

Edwards believed, in part, that God was wrathful and impatient
toward sinners and ready to kick butt, so to speak. Later revivalists of

the era following the Civil War were more likely to emphasize God's love and mercy as reasons to live the Christian life.

The background for Henry and Charlotte Quiner (Ma and Pa Quiner) was much the same, except that during their migrations they spent time in Connecticut, Ohio, and Illinois before ending up near Pepin, Wisconsin, which is near the border with Minnesota.

The Quiner and Ingalls families were neighbors, which most likely explains how Caroline and Charles met. They were married on February 1, 1860, in Pepin and were still residing there when their first child, Mary, was born in 1865. Laura came next on February 7, 1867.

Later in the family's story the Congregational Church was to become a happy home for both Charles and Caroline Ingalls, but during these years in Pepin we know only of a Methodist church in the town.

What we do know is that Pa and Ma and the girls lived about seven miles from town, and it is unlikely any formal Christian schooling began there. More likely Pa played the music for the hymns they learned, and Ma likely conducted Bible study and helped the girls memorize Scripture verses. Over time Laura learned by heart over a hundred Bible verses.

Ma was a gentle instructor and wanted her children to be good, both in the sense of being obedient, as well as acting properly, as was expected of young ladies. She applied that old rule that said women had the responsibility for maintaining community standards for sobriety and honesty. Some men thought that feminine nature civilized their "natural" unruliness.

We have the Little House books themselves to testify to these goals. Laura is told not to be selfish but to share her doll with others. Mary gets away with a certain amount of meanness by knowing just how to play the game of being good, but she torments Laura about her plain brown hair and bosses her around. Mary is also good at not being caught, but Laura is never very good at hiding her misbehavior.

In *Little House in the Big Woods,* Laura rebels against all the rules connected with Sunday. In fact, she declares that she hates Sunday. This is a pretty bold statement for any child of that age to make, and Pa has to gather Laura tenderly to himself and tell her of how his own father and his brothers had disobeyed and snuck out on a Sunday to play on a sled. A squealing pig gave away the misdeed when they struck it as they were careening down a hill. They were caught in the act, and the punishment followed.

Pa tells Laura that those times in his youth were even stricter for girls, who weren't allowed to run outside and play at all. When Laura falls asleep, it is to the sound of her father's fiddle playing hymns such as "Rock of Ages." His counsel has given her at least some comfort.

Laura was what I would call "God conscious" from early on in her life. From Laura Ingalls Wilder's manuscript entitled *Pioneer Girl,* edited by Pamela Smith Hill, we learn that Laura as a child was warned of the dangers of licking icicles—one might fall on a girl's head and injure her. Laura at first obeyed the rule but gave in little by little until she licked an icicle and then felt terribly guilty about it because she had disobeyed Ma. Her heart ached for days over what she had done before she finally confessed to Ma. Here's what happened next, as quoted in *Pioneer Girl:*

> It was such a comfort to tell her [Ma] all about it. She smoothed
> my hair and said of course she would forgive me, because I had
> told her I was sorry and that now I must say a little prayer and
> ask God to forgive me too. She told me to say "Dear God please

forgive me for telling a lie?" [*sic*] And when I did, Ma said she was sure I would never be so naughty again, then she tucked me in kissed me and went away. The fiddle was singing again as I went to sleep.

In 1868 when Laura was just a year old, the family moved from Wisconsin to Kansas Territory. Since Laura was still so young, Ma and Pa would have continued to guide her spiritual formation. In fact, all the information we have on this time comes from the memories of Pa and Ma, who related them later to Laura when she could understand them.

Sundays would have been observed at home, as they lived thirteen miles from the nearest town of Independence, Kansas. The "now I lay me down to sleep" prayers would have been said to the sound of coyotes barking and wolves howling in the company of the lonely dark. The fact is, the struggles inherent in the pioneer life tended to drive most folk to a dependence on God. It aided in character development to have a little fear of the wild. One wanted to be independent and to achieve success, but it helped when a neighbor was handy. The elements of nature were certainly out of one's control, and a thunderstorm or prairie downpour was often thought of as a frightening act of God.

I do not mean to suggest by all this that the little family on the prairie was perfect. Hardly. They shared the same prejudice toward the Native Americans as did many other settlers. And it would have been advanced religious thinking indeed for them to realize the European and the true American were brothers under the skin. Here and there an occasional missionary might speak against injustices to the Indians. Indeed, a number of Office of Indian Affairs agents spoke up against the way their "charges" were treated.

But the doctrine of Manifest Destiny—that the white man had a right to all the territory across America to the Pacific—was well established. Laura and Mary were instructed to never let their dog, Jack, loose when Indians were around, but we never hear Pa saying they should never have moved into Indian Territory in the first place. No, I'm afraid many a pioneer felt that God must be white or like Holman Hunt's painting of the time, which showed a rather Gentile-looking Christ knocking at heart's door.

Naturally, the pioneers sought the help of God, even though their choice to move and live in an often harsh frontier environment was the reason they were in harm's way. Certainly, the beloved hymns of the nineteenth century reminded them that God was a defense and shelter, and Pa would have played many a tune on his fiddle to keep the spirits of his family up.

Pa had his hopes. He was certainly counting on the government to declare the Indian land open to settlement, and history would have led him to believe this would happen, so his wait-and-see attitude made some sense.

At their crude cabin in Indian Territory, the family was too far away from Independence to visit, except to gather supplies. That journey was always made by Pa. Ma Ingalls and the children were left virtually isolated from civilization. A twenty-six-mile round trip with three small children (Carrie was born there in 1870) would have been nearly impossible and certainly not undertaken on a weekly basis to attend church.

Even if Ma and Pa could have made the trip, the churches in Independence—most likely Methodist or Baptist—might not have been a good fit for them. At this point in their lives, Methodism might well have been a bit too emotional, and the Baptist faith just hadn't been in their past experience at all. (Ironically, in later life Laura did become a Methodist, but her appreciation for privacy in religious expression never changed.)

The Family That Makes Music Together Stays Together

The Ingalls family most likely found emotional release from the tensions of their frontier situation in the old hymns of the church. The songs of a writer like Charles Wesley would have indeed provided a welcome relief and been found in any hymnal. Familiar verses such as these, from various hymns, would have brought much comfort and encouragement:

> O for a thousand tongues to sing
> My great Redeemer's praise.

> Love divine, all loves excelling,
> Joy of heaven to earth come down.

> And can it be that I should gain
> An interest in the Savior's blood?

The certainties of one's heavenly home go far when each new day can bring new peril. *Little House on the Prairie* tells of one instance when the family was awakened by the terrible screams of a panther prowling near the Verdigris River. Pa's singing helped calm his family's fears.

Dr. Dale Cockrell, former Vanderbilt professor of musicology and American and southern studies, has noted that music from Pa's fiddle played a key role in developing the Ingalls family's identity and unity. In *The Happy Land Companion,* written to supplement information for his CDs containing songs sung by the Ingalls family, he reported that there are at least 126 songs in the Little House series, with references to hundreds of other tunes scattered throughout the eight books. He noted,

> There are parlor songs, stage songs, minstrel show songs, patriotic songs, Scottish and Irish songs, hymns, spirituals, fiddle tunes, singing school songs, play party songs, folk songs, a Child ballad, broadside ballads, Christmas songs, catches and rounds, and references to "cowboy songs" and "Osage war dances." Throughout, the guiding musical spirit is her father Charles Ingalls (1835–1902), a musician who passed up few opportunities to sing and play his fiddle. It is "Pa's fiddle," carefully wrapped, stowed in its fiddle-box and cushioned by pillows, that accompanies the Ingalls family through all its adventures and comes to symbolize the endurance of the family unit in an often wild and threatening frontier world.

As the family camped on the Kansas prairie, waiting to see if the Osage Indians would agree to release their land to the American government, Pa kept the family singing. Hymns gave promise of rest and security, if not now, then "In the Sweet By and By."

> There's a land that is fairer than day,
> And by faith we can see it afar;
> For the Father waits over the way
> To prepare us a dwelling place there.

In the sweet by and by
We shall meet on that beautiful shore;
In the sweet by and by
We shall meet on that beautiful shore.

On the lighter side, Pa seems to have been the merry prankster of the family, and he used his extensive fiddle repertoire to keep family spirits high. The humorous tune "The Arkansas Traveler" is referenced in more than one Little House book. It was certainly played during their Kansas sojourn, for it was one of Pa's favorite comedic tunes.

The music itself has no words, but the accompanying story, which is related when the fiddler pauses, tells of a weary traveler who needs shelter during a rainy night. When he asks a man living in an old shack for directions to the nearest town, the homeowner tells him he's never been that way and doesn't know what lies beyond. When the traveler notices that the shack is leaking in every corner, he asks the owner why he doesn't fix the roof. The owner replies that he doesn't need to fix it when it isn't raining and to fix it when it *is* raining is foolish. The dialogue goes on like this until at last the weary traveler moves on.

Perhaps the most-played lighthearted melody of the time was "Captain Jinks." The song is referenced many times in Laura's remembrance of pioneer days. Interestingly enough, for such a religious family, the Ingallses rejoiced at Captain Jinks, who seemed to have no scruples at all.

Jinks at first admits that he feeds "[his] horse on corn and beans and sport[s] young ladies in their 'teens," though he is too old to be anybody's beau. By the second verse we find out he's "not cut out for the army" because he can't stand the discipline. He also admits to disgracefully having run from the enemy in battle. And his officers want to "kick him out of the army."

However, Jinks gets the last word: "Gentlemen! Kick me out! That's a very good joke, upon my word; I'll retire without being kicked out, and with the most profound reciprocity of feeling, you will ever find me Yours very truly," and then he sings his outlandish chorus again.

I regret that this song was not a part of my own family's repertoire, because Mom could play the piano quite well, and it would have been a favorite.

At the conclusion of *Little House on the Prairie,* the army acts by moving the settlers off of Osage Indian land. This was one of the few times when our federal government actually honored a treaty with the Indians—at least temporarily. Within another year, Washington, DC, reversed course and moved the Osage elsewhere.

In any case, Pa did not wait to be thrown off Indian land but in 1871 defiantly left the little cabin he had built (a replica now stands in its place near Independence) and moved the family once more.

The Ingalls family pilgrimage was not over. In fact, it was barely begun.

Still Looking for the Promised Land

*Laura could not say what she meant, but to her the
Wessington Hills were more than grassy hills. Their
shadowy outlines drew her with the lure of far places.*

—LAURA INGALLS WILDER

We love Laura and her family because they showed so much spunk. Being down and out in Kansas did not stop them. The Little House narrative has them going directly from Kansas to Walnut Grove, Minnesota, but in truth they returned to their home in Pepin, Wisconsin, for a brief sojourn of less than three years. There they found the big woods even more crowded and the wild game even scarcer. It didn't take them long before they packed up once again to find a future elsewhere.

Go West, Young Family, Go West

I am not entirely certain why the family came to settle on the banks of Plum Creek (still called that to this day) near Walnut Grove in 1874.

They had begun their new journey in company with Charles's brother Peter and his wife, Eliza, but that family traveled only a little way into Minnesota before settling near the Zumbro River. So the Ingallses journeyed on alone until they reached wide-open spaces in the western part of the state.

The land around Plum Creek certainly looked promising for wheat, and a single harvested crop, if the prices for grain remained good, could practically take a farmer out of debt. Two good years in a row could have him headed toward prosperity. Unfortunately, this simple scenario seldom worked out in real life.

Perhaps the Ingallses were just buoyed by being in a new place. Pa really was the wanderer; it was Ma who always wanted to settle down. Here, near Walnut Grove, there would be an opportunity of school for the girls and church fellowship together as a family for the first time. Astonishingly Pa was able to obtain 172 acres of land for a payment of only $430. (By way of comparison, my own father tried to dairy farm on only eighty acres that was mortgaged to the hilt. And at one time he had some fifty cows to care for!)

Interestingly Laura's picture of her family is still pretty much one of isolation. The Nelsons, who lived across the creek from them and were wonderful neighbors, had come all the way from Norway and could speak little English. Therefore, Ma still didn't have much company and only the help of her girls.

I believe it was about this time that the Ingalls family became involved in trying to start a church under the guidance of the Reverend Edwin Alden of the Congregational denomination. Reverend Alden was commissioned by the Home Mission Society to extend his work in eastern Minnesota at Waseca through a mission plant one hundred miles to the west in Walnut Grove. This town was growing because it lay along the path of the railway. Some towns grew and some towns didn't, but if you could catch one with an expanding population, it helped to be one of the first churches established there.

As a church planter, Reverend Alden was blessed with a cheerful disposition, and the entire Ingalls family took to him as a brother. Indeed, the words *brother* and *sister* were often used during those times to refer to fellow believers in the Lord. You still hear, in some churches, references to Brother Bob or Sister Susan, though those practices are rarer now.

Pa and Ma would have been on somewhat familiar religious ground from their childhood training, and they would have understood the church culture with which they were uniting.

Pa, as one of the founding members of Union Congregational Church, would sit in the front among the "graybeards" during the worship service, separated from Ma and his daughters. Other married men, less involved, would sit with their families. Often younger men on the lookout to see which young ladies were attending would sit in the back. Although some churches still separated the men and women of the congregation altogether, the Union church did not. Pioneering had brought some equality of pew seating to the congregations in the West.

On the whole, church was definitely planned by adults for adults, with little thought being given to the attention span of children. There was less of an effort to explain what goes on in a service than there is today. A separate "children's church" was unheard of.

So when Laura first goes to church, as recounted in *On the Banks of Plum Creek,* it comes as a bit of a shock to her. On the ride home she is asked by Pa what she thinks of church, and she doesn't quite know what to say. Then she blurts out that the people don't know how to sing very well. Pa laughs and suggests that maybe the congregation would have sung better if there were hymnbooks, but there is no money for such books right now.

Reverend Alden makes a positive impression on Laura because he takes the trouble to notice her and, we assume, Mary. Suddenly, Laura wants to go to church because she knows he will be there. She now considers her pastor a gentle man, a shepherd who loves his flock.

Notwithstanding this opinion, she honestly finds his prayers long and herself distracted during the service until she becomes interested in Sunday school. From that important time in Laura's spiritual growth comes this account from Pamela Smith Hill's *Pioneer Girl:*

> All that winter we all went to our church and Sunday-school on Sunday morning and in the afternoon I went to the Methodist church and Sunday-school.
>
> Mary did not go in the afternoon, because she was not very well all winter. Sometimes Pa went with me but I never failed because there was a contest in the Sunday-school. A prize was offered to the pupil who at the end of the year could repeat from memory, in their proper order, all the Golden Texts and Central Truths for the entire year, which would be two Bible verses for each Sunday of the year. When the time came for the test, we stood up one at a time before the whole Sunday-school and beginning with the first lesson of the year repeated first the Golden Text then the Central Truth of each lesson, one after the other as they came, without any prompting or help of any kind. The prize was a reference Bible.
>
> One after the other they tried and failed until my turn came and I was perfect. But alas so was Howard Ensign when

his turn came and there were both of us winners with only one prize between us.

My teacher, the preacher's wife, said if I would wait until she could send and get another Bible she would get me one with a clasp, so I was glad to wait.

Howard Ensign had joined the Congregational church after their revival and would testify at prayer meeting every Wednesday night. It someway offended my sense of privacy. It seemed to me that the things between one and God should be between him and God like loving ones [*sic*] mother. One didn't go around saying "I love my mother, she has been so good to me." One just loved her and did things that she liked one to do.

At this stage in Laura's faith journey, I believe the church's real ministry was to reinforce what she was already being taught at home. Of course she memorized Scripture because that is what Ma had taught her to do. Of course she obeyed Pa because the commandments said to honor your father and mother. Of course she wanted to be good because virtue is its own reward.

The truth is, without that early Sunday school experience at Union Congregational Church and at the Methodist meetings, church might well have palled for Laura, who was not always a ready listener but more of an active tomboy. She learned at church because she was learning at home, where she could see real faith lived out, and Sunday school was interactive enough to use up some of her excess energy.

One of the astonishing things about both Pa and Ma during this period of their children's development is that they actually listened to their children. While Laura often depicted herself as being angry with her parents—because they always believed Mary's version of events over Laura's version when the two sisters fought—she also admitted that both Pa and Ma listened to her with kindness when she came to them with her troubles.

For example, when Laura disobeys Pa and tries to go to the Plum Creek swimming hole alone, she knows she has done wrong. She goes to Pa and confesses her evil intentions to disobey the rule. Instead of quickly scolding her, as many of us would do, Pa listens to her and admits he doesn't quite know what to say. If she is going to disobey, he can't trust her, and yet he can't follow her around all the time either. Finally, he decides she will be confined to their dugout home for a day. If Ma reports that she has been good and has done her chores, freedom to run around outside will be restored.

Thus, Laura receives restoration and a valuable lesson. This is certainly a theme that runs throughout her books, for we find she always berates herself in comparison with Mary. Pa and Ma can only assure her that she really is their reliable little daughter—with the brown, not the blond, hair. Mary, who was blond, always said blond is prettier. As a boy, it was a relief for me to discover in *On the Banks of Plum Creek* that Mary didn't always obey either. I was getting weary of Mary's perfection too.

Walnut Grove was such an important place for Laura. There was not just the town itself but the creek and the cows and the church—and the nasty Nellie Oleson. As an adult Laura admitted on a number of occasions that Nellie, as a character in her writing, was a composite person made up of several girls who had crossed swords with her from time to time. Yet this composite Nellie was so real to Laura that, even decades later, she often referred to Nellie as though she were really just one person.

Nellie is depicted as being a store owner's daughter who has everything Laura ever coveted, and she is a recurring character in Laura's narrative because she serves as a useful reminder of just how poor the Ingalls family was and how envy can dwell in even the humblest home. Nellie has dolls and candy and the snobbery of someone who doesn't have to do any chores.

Nellie's character is included in a Christmas story that teaches Laura much about the need to receive charity when charity is offered. As the story is told, Reverend Alden decides there will be a real Christmas celebration at the mission church, even though the congregation as a whole is struggling to make ends meet. A tree is brought in, and the folks back east send candy and other items for the settlers. The warmth and the glow of this event foreshadow the poverty that is slowly engulfing the Ingallses. Crops have failed, grasshoppers have come, and the rain has disappeared—the realities of pioneering are much on display—but the church is still a light in the darkness. With a scraggly tree decorated with presents literally hung from its branches, celebration comes even when there is pain and sorrow.

Laura leaves this event filled with joy. She is almost willing to forgive Nellie for being Nellie since Laura has gotten just the presents she had wanted, a little fur muff and a cape.

Strange Interlude

The brave little family pulled out of Walnut Grove to go to a town to the east, Burr Oak, Iowa, in 1876. A son, Charles Frederick Ingalls, had been born in 1875, a light and a hope for his parents, who needed a boy to help Pa in his farming. But the lad was sickly. On the way from Walnut Grove to Burr Oak, he died and was buried near South Troy,

Minnesota, close to where Pa's brother Peter and his family were living. After that Pa and the family stayed with his brother for a while, and then Pa moved on to his new, but certainly not welcome, job as a clerk at the Masters Hotel in Burr Oak. Later, when the family followed, they all stayed with the Steadmans, who had also backtracked from Walnut Grove. The Steadmans seem to have been principal owners of the property, but the Ingalls family treated it as a joint venture.

Although sometimes the way forward requires a retreat, Laura appears to have felt unable to write about this time in her family's fortunes. The time in Burr Oak is not covered in the Little House books. We know of the episode only from the history left by Laura's letters and manuscripts, and the references to the family made by Burr Oak descendants.

Things weren't all dark in the town, and there was a church there. The Congregationalists were established, but we know nothing of how the family was involved—if at all—with the church. Pa kept their hopes up by playing his fiddle, and Ma continued to drill the girls in their knowledge of the Bible. And the town school greatly improved Laura's reading skills, as she remembered years later.

The truth is that Pa and Ma worked very hard to make a go of it in Iowa. The hotel was a busy place, and their daughters were put to work helping where they could. Besides clerking, Pa did odd jobs about the town, helped at a grinding mill, and turned a hand at carpentry. No one could accuse him of being a lazy man, and he tried to keep his hopes up for Ma and the girls' sake.

But Ma quickly had the family moved from the hotel because of the rowdiness of some of the guests. A man had once shot at his wife there, and there were bullet holes above a door to remind them of the event. The town also had a saloon, and Ma certainly did not approve of that. A man had once drunk so much alcohol that when he lit a match for a smoke, his breath caught fire and he died!

No, even though baby Grace was born in Burr Oak in 1877, the family wanted to forget they ever lived there. Before that experience was over, a neighbor lady had tried to adopt Laura (Laura was horrified), and Pa had to load the family in the wagon at night so they could escape while owing debts, which I believe Pa later paid, though he had threatened not to do so.

So it was back to Walnut Grove and more friendly territory.

Go West, Young Family—Again

The family's first real hometown offered the same promises and challenges as before, and they were again in a place that felt much more like home than Burr Oak ever had. They were in the magical West of Pa's dreams.

Mary was blind now. The onset of her blindness had been gradual, and they could only speculate on the nature of what caused it. The word *typhoid* has been used to explain Mary's fever, which is told about in *By the Shores of Silver Lake,* but other authorities have diagnosed a bad case of measles as the problem. Still others have concluded that Mary suffered from a neurological illness. In any case, the adult Mrs. Wilder couldn't find the right words to describe the illness. It just came, and the blindness resulted. Laura would have preferred to just blot out that time altogether. There are things you'd like to forget to give your heart a break.

Church and Christian fellowship in Walnut Grove meant more than ever to them. They renewed their ties with old friends and met new ones who had come to settle. Grasshoppers were still a problem, and farming was still risky, but the pioneer West gave a man the opportunity to try and try again. At least in that way the frontier was forgiving.

Pa was immediately elected a trustee of the Union Congregational Church and took his appointed place in the pews. Blind Mary is also specifically recorded as a member, but records are incomplete, for surely Ma was a member along with her husband or else he could not have been elected to his office.

Laura was active again in Sunday school and church, pretty much in that order, and it is probably around this time that she began to witness the experience of pioneer revival meetings. Frankly, she found them scary and off putting. Kindly Reverend Alden was no longer at the church, and another minister now filled the pulpit.

It was all a bit overwhelming at these revival services. Laura's hair would rise on the back of her head, and chills would run up and down her spine. A terrifying emotionalism seemed to creep into the services and take possession of the church. The minister's words no longer seemed to make any sense and were a jumble of exhortation and warning. In her imagination the preacher almost seemed to turn into the devil himself as he carried on, shouting in the pulpit. Then the special meetings would be over and life would settle down again.

Still, it was not the same old Walnut Grove. People kept coming and going, and Pa continued to show that he was a man of many talents—and he needed to be. He did not farm again on this second sojourn but ran his own butcher shop and did any carpentry he could pick up. People were continually building in a new territory.

The economy did not always boom and there was no government safety net, but if a man could work, there was usually something he could do. The trouble was in finding something at which one might really prosper.

Fortunately, the Chicago and North Western Railroad ran through the town, and it was extending into Dakota Territory. Dr. John Miller, in his *Becoming Laura Ingalls Wilder*, said that "Charles's sister Ladocia offered an opportunity to him." Her husband, Hiram, was a contractor and knew of an opening. Pa was to work at a railroad camp on the edge of a new settlement for fifty dollars a month, which was a significant salary for those days when the average cowboy made only about thirty for the month. And there would be a place for him to stay.

Being unencumbered with having to sell a farmstead or any significant property, Charles accepted the job and in no time had his family on the road toward Silver Lake in Dakota Territory.

It helps in the moving on to have next to nothing to carry with you.

Finally, Home on the Prairie

Laura tells us all about Pa's time with the railroad near Silver Lake and of her growth toward womanhood, but a real dividing line in her life from girlhood to becoming a young woman comes with being involved in the founding of De Smet, South Dakota, the Little Town on the Prairie.

As for church, her father and others helped Reverend Alden found another mission work, which was later incorporated as the First Congregational Church under the leadership of the Reverend Edward Brown in 1880.

Laura always believed that somehow the beloved Reverend Alden had been cheated out of his place as this church's first pastor. She regarded Reverend Brown as looking something like a wild man with raggedy clothes and an unkempt beard stained by tobacco juice.

However, later she became close friends with Ida Brown, Reverend Brown's daughter, and she also wrote an appreciation of Mrs. Brown for the *Missouri Ruralist* after she began her column with that paper.

For some reason Laura must not have had a letter of membership from a previous church, so only Pa, Ma, and Mary are listed as founding members, joining "by letter from other churches." When the church was formally incorporated a few months later, Pa was again elected as a trustee, so he can be said to have helped in the founding of two churches.

The whole family became deeply involved in First Congregational activities, and reports from local papers indicate that a number of churches of different denominations helped each other get started. When meeting places were in short supply, an Episcopal service was held at a Baptist church, and even a Catholic church was helped to get a start in a town primarily filled with Protestants. It was also the custom in De Smet to have "union" services where different groups would get together for mutual worship.

At about the age of fifteen, Laura began to notice the attention of men, hapless bachelors who had settled in a town without many eligible women. Some of the men spent their time in the saloon, but Almanzo James Wilder made his way to church and soon found a way to escort Laura home, even though her family was living in De Smet for the winter and their house was only a few blocks from the church.

Interestingly enough, all we know about Almanzo's church background from Malone, New York, near where he grew up, is that the Sabbath was strictly kept, the sermons were two hours long, and little boys were expected to sit and remain quiet all day.

Laura and Almanzo's romance and marriage are thoroughly covered in the last books of her children's series, but before she ever thought of him as marriage material, he became her Sunday rescuer when at only fifteen she began her teaching career at the Brewster School.

The school term lasted only two months of the winter and paid twenty dollars a month, but the work was true labor for someone so young. She boarded with the Brewster family, and in my opinion, the unhappy woman of the house—Mrs. Brewster—was clinically depressed and wanted her husband to give up farming. Mrs. Brewster's open quarreling and criticizing of her husband shocked Laura and made her want to run home to the comfort of Ma and Pa, who would never do such things.

With horses and sleigh, Almanzo began making the twelve-mile drive when he sensed how much she hated staying at the Brewster home. She in particular remembered one Christmas that her future husband made so special:

This was my first school . . . but I was only sixteen [*sic*] years old and twelve miles from home during a frontier winter. I walked a mile over the unbroken snow from my boarding place to school every morning and back at night. There were only a few pupils, and on this particular snowy afternoon, they were restless, for it was nearing 4 o'clock and tomorrow was Christmas. "Teacher" was restless too, though she tried not to show it, for she was wondering if she could get home for Christmas Day.

It was almost too cold to hope for Father to come, and a storm was hanging in the northwest which might mean a blizzard at any minute. Still, tomorrow was Christmas—and then there was a jingle of sleigh bells outside. A man in a huge fur coat in a sleigh full of robes passed the window. I was going home after all! . . .

I'll never forget that ride. The bells made a merry jingle, and the fur robes were warm; but the weather was growing colder, and the snow was drifting so that the horses must break their way through the drifts.

We were facing the strong wind, and every little while he, who later became the "Man of the Place" [Laura's title for her husband], must stop the team, get out in the snow, and by putting his hands over each horse's nose in turn, thaw the ice from them where the breath had frozen over their nostrils. Then he would get back into the sleigh, and on we'd go until once more the horses could not breathe for the ice.

When we reached the journey's end, it was 40 degrees below zero; the snow was blowing so thickly that we could not see across the street; and I was so chilled that I had to be half carried into the house. But I was home for Christmas, and cold and danger were forgotten.

Go South, Young Family, Go South

Laura and Almanzo were married at the home of Reverend Brown in August 1885, and they remained together until Almanzo passed away sixty-four years later. They were not married in a church because Almanzo had pushed up the date of their marriage to keep his sister and mother from interfering by planning a big wedding, which he could not afford, and—by his estimation—ruining their special day.

By this time Laura and Almanzo had been going together for three years, so the decision was not hasty nor made on a whim. Honeymoons were an unheard of thing; they got right down to living in their own little home that Manly—for that was one of Laura's names for her husband—built for her.

Laura was called Bessie because Manly had a sister Laura with whom he did not get along. Laura had said the name Almanzo presented its own difficulties, and so they compromised. Odd, but compromise is a good beginning for any marriage.

A chronology of their early years together reads like an epic Greek tragedy.

1885—Laura and Almanzo are married.

1886—Daughter Rose is born.

1887—Laura's father has to give up on his claim and move to town.

1888—Laura and Almanzo become ill with what is labeled diphtheria. But later, while recovering, Almanzo has a stroke from which he is slow to recover. He walks with a limp for the rest of his life.

1888—Laura and Almanzo lose a boy child who lives only twelve days. He is buried unnamed. Rose did not learn until years later—well into her adulthood—that she once had a brother.

1889—The couple's house burns down.

1890—Laura and Almanzo and daughter Rose move to Spring Valley, Minnesota, to live with Almanzo's parents while he continues to recover from his stroke.

1891—Laura and Almanzo move to Florida to see if a change in climate will help Almanzo.

1892—The family moves back to De Smet, where Laura can
work and bring in a little money.
1894—Life starts over again. The family moves to the Ozarks
of Missouri.

Trials of faith send you in new directions you never thought of
before.

Going to the Promised Land

The best account of Laura, Almanzo, and Rose's trip to Mansfield,
Missouri, is recorded in Laura's book *On the Way Home,* a marvelous
record of a desperate journey. Laura and Almanzo had been married
just nine years, and many modern marriages probably would not have
survived the disasters they had been through.

The reason for choosing Missouri was that a railroad brochure they
had seen referred to the Ozarks, and the area around Mansfield in particular, as the "land of big red apples." This promise of abundance and
a milder climate prompted them and their friends the Cooleys to try
one more time for a promised land.

With them went a hundred-dollar bill, all the money that Laura
and Almanzo had managed to save for this one last attempt at security
and a home, and this bill was tucked in a hidden place in Laura's lap
desk until it would be needed for a down payment on Ozark land.

If you read Laura's account, you will be amazed by the variety of
settlements they passed through. On the journey Almanzo traded fire
mats made out of a new material called asbestos for food and supplies,
and Laura kept careful account in a diary, some of her first real writing,
though not for the public at that time.

By August 1894 they had arrived, but the hundred-dollar bill was missing! Rose, who edited *On the Way Home* and added some material of her own, many years later recounted in the book's last chapter the story of the missing money. You can just feel the horror of the experience.

Had the money fallen out of the desk? Laura had last seen it in Kansas.

Had their friends the Cooleys taken it? No, that was impossible.

Had Rose been playing with the desk? "No!" was her emphatic reply.

Weeks went by. Laura had fallen in love with some hill land with seedling apple trees laid out on it, ready to be planted, but with the hundred-dollar bill missing, no down payment could be made. There were more searches of the desk and still nothing.

Almanzo began to look for odd jobs about town.

Then Laura looked one last time in the desk—and there the bill was. The joy could hardly be described.

Life begins just about the time you think it is over. They had their farm, and they never left it.

And someday Laura would have remarkable stories to tell.

Partners in Faith

Lay not up for yourselves treasures upon earth, where
moth and rust doth corrupt, and where thieves break
through and steal: but lay up for yourselves treasures in
heaven, where neither moth nor rust doth corrupt, and
where thieves do not break through nor steal.

—MATTHEW 6:19–20

I believe Almanzo would have found his way to church anyway,
but being married to Laura definitely made it easier for him to
become an active member in the churches they attended in De Smet
and Mansfield. There are a multitude of reasons why a farmer might
excuse himself from the duty of being active in a fellowship, but they
all amount to the same thing in the end: the Sabbath is one more day
for him to get his work done on the homestead—and be out in God's
great green church of nature.

What Was Almanzo Like?

The Reverend Carleton Knight, one of the Wilders' Methodist pastors
in Mansfield, once commented that Almanzo was "shy of preachers."

But this characterization was made of Almanzo in his eighties. By that time some neighborhood boys thought of him as a recluse. We do know that Laura and Almanzo considered church attendance to be a regular part of their lives and a normal Sunday activity from their youth onward. Laura certainly attended church out of conviction.

In *Farmer Boy,* Laura's book on Almanzo's boyhood, devoutness of habit both in the family and in the culture meant that while there was rest from labor, Sunday was also the most boring day of the week. Quite frankly, it was a hated day for many children, a day of abstention, a day of self-denial from anything that might be fun. You'd best use the day to catch a nap so that the day might go quickly. It is hard to know how much damage is done to the religion of Jesus—who once was observed to be "eating and drinking, . . . gluttonous, and a winebibber, a friend of publicans and sinners"—by those whose path to holiness is achieved by denying every pleasure.

Later in the Little House series, Almanzo gets to escort Laura home from church, and that is the first time Laura realizes she has a beau. She is mortified by this discovery since she regards Almanzo as a grown man while she is still a girl of fifteen. Indeed, Almanzo was twenty-five, and the difference in age was a trial to both of them at first.

The Family's Faith

During the first ten years of their married life, Laura and Almanzo's faith must have been strongly tested. As noted earlier, among the family's disasters were a house fire, numerous crop failures, the loss of a son—who was never named—a battle with diphtheria that weakened both of them, terrible bank debt, and Almanzo's subsequent stroke that left him crippled in one foot. His recovery was achingly slow. Laura had to take on a heavy load.

Of course, the young couple didn't struggle alone. Everyone suffered from the same failed crops and the same high prices for basic goods that could only be brought from the East. Other children died of mysterious, untreatable diseases. It could be said that it was a rare family indeed who did not lose a child or suffer from a life-threatening illness. Also, considerable livestock perished due to disease and bad weather. Many pioneers could only live in a kind of hopeful poverty that said, "Things will be better next year."

During the first years of their marriage, Laura and Almanzo would have regularly attended the De Smet Congregational church. Reverend Brown had retired, having come to his last pastorate late in life. He himself was a homesteader with a claim to work, and his son Mark had a stake in the local newspaper. But even with the formidable Reverend Brown retired and gone, there would have been interruptions to Laura and Almanzo's attendance at the De Smet church, for they had left for Spring Valley, Minnesota, and then for Florida to see if a southern climate would improve Almanzo's health. In fact, I suspect they were not able to reconnect with church and church friends until they moved back to De Smet after their fruitless year living in the South. Upon their return to De Smet, they stayed, for a time, with Laura's family until Almanzo could literally get back on his feet.

But recover they did, slowly. Almanzo worked odd jobs around town and Laura did sewing work until the couple had amassed one hundred dollars with which to make a new beginning near Mansfield in the Missouri Ozarks, a town suggested to them by friends who were going there also.

On finding no Congregational church in Mansfield in 1894, when they first arrived, Laura and Almanzo became active in the Methodist church there. Historian William Anderson noted that the church was already organized by that time, but in an interview for a history of the church in the 1950s, Laura remembered a building dedication that was held in 1900. So perhaps the Wilders moved to new facilities only six years after their arrival. The town would have been growing through immigration at that time: the Ozark climate was so much better than northern winters.

As someone already familiar with Methodism, Mrs. Wilder would have enlisted and been active in the Ladies Aid Society. Women in pioneer churches often took leadership roles without receiving official titles of recognition for their contributions, and Laura was an involved church member, such as her mother had been. Since the couple lived nearly a full mile outside of town—in a rude cabin much like the one in *Little House on the Prairie*—they might not have been as active as the townsfolk. And I don't think one can say that Almanzo was ever as active as Pa was in shepherding his children's spiritual life. But daughter Rose wasn't a sheep to be led easily. Still, church would have offered considerable entertainment in the form of singing and socializing, with no competition from modern media options.

Other denominations in the area would have been Catholic, Baptist, and Presbyterian. There would have been several kinds of Baptists, and Mrs. Wilder spoke favorably of those who washed each other's feet as part of their ceremonies. Doctrinal distinctions would have made for an abundance of different groups in this settled community. However, there would have been a general agreement among these groups that a person needed to have a personal relationship with Jesus Christ, who was received by faith as God's one and only sacrifice for our sin. Some churches would have offered calls to come forward as a show of public witness that a person was committing her life to Jesus Christ and receiving him into her heart by faith.

To have done all this in one fell swoop of commitment would have required a seeker to already know a fair amount of teaching from the Gospels and the Epistles of the New Testament—and to have seen a few others go forward before one felt so moved. Hence, attendance at Sunday school, where one received such teaching, would have been important for both adults and children.

Just such a teacher was Mr. A. C. Barton, who came to Laura's attention as a man who practiced what he'd been taught. In fact, he was a Methodist lay preacher who occasionally filled pulpit vacancies. He also was a farmer and had a twenty-five-acre farm to sustain himself and his family. Laura approved of his type of practical Christianity.

She wrote of Mr. Barton in a *Ruralist* article, saying that he may have had a call to "Go Preach Christ" or it could have been a call to "Go Plow Corn." In any case, she approved of his "agricultural theology." Barton believed that "robbing the soil is sin, and that like every other sin it brings its own punishment." You don't go looking for a better place to live, she concluded. You make one where you are. Almanzo was that type of practical man.

In fact, I wonder if it wasn't just such an appreciation of practicality that led both Laura and Almanzo to become Masons. Masonic activity was pervasive all throughout the Midwest at this time, and Pa and Ma had been early Masons in De Smet. The Wilders' own association with a lodge might have sprung from that time in their lives.

Although the Masonic culture had its religious elements, it was also just another organization to which a person might belong for the doing of good works. Pa had also belonged to the Odd Fellows lodge, which promoted the temperance cause as its main mission.

Perhaps the thing to keep in mind about both Laura and Almanzo is that neither one was keen on religious controversy or doctrinal hairsplitting. Laura could speak approvingly of the practice of washing one another's feet without ever wanting to be a foot washer herself. In any case, the people around them would have held similar religious beliefs. A community of new and old settlers could be quite homogenous really, except maybe in conflicts over when and in what mode to baptize.

The Methodists' singular contribution to community life would have been the camp meeting, held either as a weeklong "vacation" or as a weekend event. For Mrs. Wilder, the singing part was special above all else because such songs had been sung at home around the hearth as Pa played his fiddle. These songs would have been familiar territory. In fact, she and Almanzo had courted partly by going to singing school, where religious songs were mixed in with fun songs such as "Three Blind Mice" and "Old MacDonald Had a Farm." In the chapter "Barnum Walks" from *These Happy Golden Years,* their songbook contained the anthem "The Heavens Declare the Glory," Christianity and social life combining to be part of everyday common experience.

Shadows on the Grass

We are told that the life of a woman on a farm is narrow
and that the monotony of it drives many farm women
insane.

—LAURA INGALLS WILDER

Ilove the books written by Laura Ingalls Wilder, but one of her
later offerings actually unsettled me when I first read it some
forty years ago. *The First Four Years* is now included in sets of the Little
House series, but when it first came out in 1971, it was a separate title,
a discovery of a continuation of Laura and Almanzo's life after *These
Happy Golden Years,* which had ended the original series. Apparently,
Laura had at least considered completing another volume. Then, supposedly, it had been put aside for good when Almanzo died at the age
of ninety-two in 1949.

The brief account that remained and was turned into a book dis-
turbed me because I had expected the same relatively cheerful tone as
the previous books. I wanted something like "east or west; home is best"
or "happy the home when God is there." Yet here, in *The First Four*

Years, was sorrow after sorrow and discouragement aplenty. The only joy was the birth of baby Rose, whom Laura's sister Grace thought the best of babies.

I slowly realized that although I had grown up with the Little House books, I really hadn't thought of what an adult's view might be of them. Might there be a more profound understanding to be gained? Was there more to the story than had been told? How had Laura responded spiritually to these trying times?

Eventually, as I read more about her and more by her—particularly in her writings for adults—I came to the conclusion that there was much more to know about Mrs. Wilder and her family than I first had considered. I needed to go deeper in my analysis of her pioneer life and faith to understand the true Laura. Thus, the need for this book that explores the culture and context of Laura's family and upbringing and how they influenced her spiritual development.

When the Sun Hides Its Face

Based on what we read in *The First Four Years,* I wonder to what extent pioneer women, in particular, battled the debilitating effects of depression. And did Laura, too, on occasion have to find ways to combat dark moods?

Fortunately, there are some sources we can examine to seek answers, thanks in part to the ambitions of Arthur Capper. Few have heard of Mr. Capper today, but at one time he was quite a mover and shaker. A man with political ambitions, he built a farm newspaper empire that made him rich and influential throughout the Midwest. He was from Kansas and was a powerful US senator from 1919 to 1949, after having served two terms as governor.

In 1910 he purchased the *Missouri Ruralist,* a periodical still published to this day, and because Laura was asked to become a writer for this publication in 1911—and to become farm and home editor around 1915—we have her firsthand, nonfiction voice from an adult perspective, enhancing our picture of her pioneer life and times.

Mrs. Wilder wrote boldly about depression in the *Ruralist,* and I think what she said throws light on a common battle for pioneer women. Here's an excerpt from a column Laura wrote in 1920:

> The whole world was a deep, dark blue, for I had waked with a grouch that morning. While blue is without doubt a heavenly color, it is better in skies than in one's mind; for when the blues descend upon a poor mortal on earth, life seems far from being worth the living.
>
> I didn't want to help with the chores; I hated to get breakfast; and the prospect of doing up the morning's work afterward was positively revolting. Beginning the usual round of duties— under protest—I had a great many thoughts about work and none of them was complimentary to the habit.

We know from other materials written about the pioneer era that the task of maintaining emotional health may have been at least as challenging as surviving the numerous threats to physical survival. This reality is profoundly revealed in the book *Giants in the Earth* by Ole E. Rölvaag, which was published in 1927. *Giants* was recognized as an instant classic, a book *Nation* magazine declared "the fullest, finest and most powerful novel that has been written about pioneer life in America." The late Columbia University historian Henry Steele Commager called *Giants* "the most penetrating and mature depictment of the

westward movement in our literature. Of all tragedies," he wrote, "the most poignant is that of futility. . . . And futility is the moral of *Giants in the Earth*."

One of the "giants" that lurked on Rölvaag's prairie was despair, revealed so powerfully in the lives of pioneer women in particular. Life on the prairie, especially for those who were homesteading a farm many miles from the nearest neighbor or small town, often brought an unrelenting isolation. The work of child-rearing and daily chores on a frontier farm was unending and exhausting—and often had to be accomplished by the wife without the encouragement and support of other women. To some extent, Laura shared this lot in life herself, and she certainly was aware of the effects of depression from her experience as a young teacher while boarding in the home of the troubled Mrs. Brewster.

And we are fortunate to have information from a contemporary of hers that affirms the emotional perils of day-to-day frontier life, although the Little House books exposed little of this reality.

Laura would have known of Neva Whaley and her family, who came to know the Ingallses at just about the time Laura was graduating from school. Neva, Mrs. Whaley's oldest daughter and a contemporary of Laura's, certainly saw firsthand that depression was more than a mere state of mind. Her mother became so sick with depression that she nearly came to the end of all hope.

It appears that Neva Whaley was plenty busy living her own story as an early settler to the very same area of Dakota as Mrs. Wilder. In a reminiscence done near her one-hundredth birthday in 1973, Mrs. Neva (Whaley) Harding, then of Brookings, South Dakota, reflected on the roots of her mother's despair and the conditions that brought it about.

One intriguing point Neva made in the memoir was that pioneering wasn't especially hard on children; they had work to do, but not so many worries. She said that a child had responsibilities and that was all, and at the age of five, her brother, Marshall, did get put to work nailing lath to the house's interior walls to keep the cold out.

As Neva observed, children easily adjusted to their environment. They had little past for comparison, lived each day as it came, and had no plans for the future. They were not as wildly happy as adults supposed, nor were they as sad. Children simply floated along and took life as they found it. Given food, warmth, and shelter, they were not critical, nor did they wonder how their parents managed to provide.

During the hard winter of 1880–81—described in Laura's *The Long Winter*—the whole Whaley family took turns rolling hay into sticks that could be used for firewood. Time passed, and the children thought this activity a normal way of life. Even during that historic winter, the children had diversions: their father, Josiah Whaley, carved wooden toys, such as monkeys on a stick that could be made to move up and down a "tree." Like Charles Ingalls, Mr. Whaley played the fiddle, so the family had music, the same tunes that Pa played: "The Arkansas Traveler," "Money Musk," and "Pop Goes the Weasel." He also made wooden guns that could fire paper wads. Neva had a doll— and one doll only—to care for. There were also marbles, dominoes, clothespins, and building blocks around. Marshall and Neva played choo choo by turning over chairs and using a quilting frame for rails. In short, they had a feeling of security in the midst of great danger.

Meanwhile, Mother Whaley worked and worked and worked— alone. This isolation apparently became a factor of her depressive state. Consider the situation of Mrs. Whaley, who was only twenty-eight when she was introduced to Laura Ingalls. Her life consisted of:

- Raising chickens
- Planting and tending a large garden, with an emphasis on potatoes
- Growing flowers: hollyhocks, pansies, rose moss, and tiger lilies
- Starting a strawberry bed
- Setting out currant and gooseberry bushes and rhubarb
- Setting trees: apple, plum, box elder, oak, walnut, ash, willow, balm of Gilead, and barberry hedge
- Watching out for prairie fires and protecting the house when they came sweeping by

None of these had to do with the other routine tasks of mending, sewing new clothes, making meals, and seeing that the children were warm, safe, and occupied with cleaning the stove, taking out the ashes, and washing the dishes. Their family had no well the first winter, having moved there after the ground had frozen, but they could use snow, which had to be melted first, of course. Homestead visiting was rare, so Mother Whaley had very few visitors.

After the hard winter of 1880–81, Mr. Whaley was able to get out of the house and walk the three miles to De Smet, where he found carpentry work—again a parallel to Pa Ingalls. De Smet is where he would have first met the Ingalls family and Pa in particular. There he would have been invited to attend the Congregational church, but for the entire five years he held his claim, he never felt prosperous enough to own a horse and buggy. Therefore, there was no way to transport himself and his family to Sunday worship, thus further contributing to his wife's isolation.

Mr. Whaley did little farming, being content to work in town. The

walk was not that far but left little time in the evenings for anything except to take care of the cow. Then he went to bed, it being impossible to read much by candlelight.

As for Mrs. Whaley, she worked on the farm around the clock. Neva recalled,

Mother's lot was to stay home all day with a couple of small children, hoe the garden, wrestle with the fleet-footed Jersey cow—one day she got the picket rope twisted about her ankle and was dragged several rods. But it was the monotony, the loneliness that was the worst. In all the five years we lived on the claim, she went to only one public entertainment, a dance at the Exchange Hotel. She seldom got off the place for even part of a day. If we had had a horse and buggy, she could have found something different to look at once in a while. If we had been building up a farm, getting stock about us and making progress, she might have felt it worthwhile. As it was, it was like putting her, at twenty-eight, into prison for the five best years of her life. It must have taken a lot out of her, too, when I was sick for so long the first summer with what was undoubtedly a burst appendix and no doctor to be had. And she grieved over the death of her youngest brother back in Illinois of typhoid; she felt if she had been with him to nurse him, he might not have died.

The despair in Mrs. Whaley's life was nearly palpable, and after battling some physical problems, she apparently descended into a time of darkest depression:

Mother regained her health but she lost her courage. She drifted into deep despondency with long spells of weeping; she continually talked to herself and kept saying she wished she were dead. I was so frightened I told her she couldn't die, she dared not leave Marsh and me all alone. She looked at me as though she had entirely forgotten who I was, sighed and said, bitterly, "No, I guess I can't even die."

Now, when people get in that condition, they are said to be having a nervous breakdown and are sent away for a complete change of scene, but in pioneer days they were said to be having the "blues" and were left to fight it out by themselves as best they could.

The five years were finally at an end, and we moved to town in time to save Mother's sanity.

In a way, this was a happy ending for Mrs. Whaley, but we should not be tempted to think that many other sufferers were able to make their way to help and restoration.

In addition to Rölvaag's *Giants in the Earth*, the reality of life for pioneer women was also revealed in the book *Let the Hurricane Roar* (later titled *Young Pioneers*), written by none other than Laura and Almanzo's own daughter, Rose Wilder Lane (she was married to but later divorced from Gillette Lane, a salesman). This book was published in 1933 at the same time Laura's *Farmer Boy* was released as her second book in the Little House series. Oh, the contrast in atmosphere between the two books!

Let the Hurricane Roar is widely regarded as Rose's best novel, and yet it is astonishingly drab in descriptive detail, whereas Laura's prairies often come to life and bloom with color. In *Let the Hurricane Roar,*

Rose simply did not bother with extraneous detail. The stark fight is against terrifying nature, and that is that. It is a gray kind of book with a gray kind of victory at the end.

In a word, *Let the Hurricane Roar* is spiritually barren too. The hope of the redeemed is missing. The book was derived right from the history of Mama Bess (the name by which Rose referred to her mother), particularly those periods as related by Laura in *On the Banks of Plum Creek, By the Shores of Silver Lake,* and *The Long Winter.* In a little over one hundred terse pages, Rose used her mother's story, and most especially that of Pa and Ma—her grandparents—to tell of a bleak prairie life that only occasionally offered hope.

The principal characters of *Let the Hurricane Roar* were borrowed or appropriated, depending on how you look at it, from the story Laura was already telling. And although homage to Rose's ancestors may have been intended, Laura was appalled at Rose's depiction of her and her parents' lives. She had her own story to tell and, at first, felt co-opted by this book of her daughter's. And when you think about it, this borrowing was a very bold thing for Rose to have done. Aunt Carrie and Aunt Grace were still living when Rose took up her grand-parents' story to use as a book, and one would think Rose would have felt obligated to ask permission from both her aunts and her mother to do what she did!

As for the story line in *Let the Hurricane Roar,* the hero and hero-ine, David and Molly, are pitted more against the malevolent forces of fate than against a mere untamed land. Rose wanted her pioneers to be free, independent souls and true to themselves. In Shakespeare's words, they "canst not then be false to any man."

The esteemed poet W. E. Henley, who expressed convictions simi-lar to Rose's, opined in his famous "Invictus,"

In the fell clutch of circumstance
    I have not winced nor cried aloud.
Under the bludgeonings of chance
    My head is bloody, but unbowed. . . .

It matters not how strait the gate,
    How charged with punishments the scroll,
I am the master of my fate;
    I am the captain of my soul.

In concluding her article in the *Ruralist* on the themes of struggle and even depression in the pioneer world—after explaining her blue mood—Laura concluded,

But presently my mind took a wider range and became less personal as applied to the day just beginning.

First, I remembered the old, old labor law, "Six days shalt thou labor, and do all thy work: But the seventh day is the Sabbath of the Lord thy God: in it thou shalt not do any work." . . .

We may not, "Remember the Sabbath day, to keep it holy," but we'll not forget to stop working. With our present attitude toward work, the emphasis should be put upon "Six days thou shalt labor," [*sic*] and if we stick it out to work the six days, we will rest on the seventh without any urging. Given half a chance, we will take Saturday off also and any other day or part of a day we can manage to sneak. . . .

I got the thrill at the moment that my mind reached the climax. . . . My hands had performed their accustomed task with none of the usual sense of unpleasantness, showing that, after all, it is not so much the work we do with our bodies that makes us tired and dissatisfied as the work we do with our minds.

Mrs. Wilder had once said in another column that it all depends on how you look at it:

Things and persons appear to us according to the light we throw upon them from our own minds. . . . What we see is always affected by the light in which we look at it. . . . You are the window through which you must see the world.

For the poet Henley, and perhaps for Laura's daughter, Rose, there may have been no higher power to assure hope. But for other pioneers, such as Laura, God became her shelter during storms, even the blue ones.

As the old hymn inspires,

Oh, Jesus is a Rock in a weary land,
A weary land, a weary land;
Oh, Jesus is a Rock in a weary land,
A Shelter in the time of storm.

A Mary and Martha Mix

"Oh, for a little time to enjoy the beauties around me,"
I thought. "Just a little while to be free of the tyranny
of things that must be done!" A feeling of bitterness
crept into my soul. "You'll have plenty of leisure
someday when you are past enjoying it," I thought.
"You know, in time, you always get what you have
longed for and when you are old and feeble and past
active use then you'll have all the leisure you ever have
wanted. But my word! You'll not enjoy it!"

I was horrified at these thoughts.

—LAURA INGALLS WILDER

As an adult, Laura may have had a few horrifying thoughts
from time to time due to her tendency to get stressed out
by the many challenges and duties of Ozark farming. As conscientious
a person as she was, this fretfulness of hers probably couldn't be helped.

Whether it was what has been called the Protestant work ethic or
just the fact that the work of a farmer's wife is never done, Laura Ingalls

Wilder always found herself struggling with wanting to be a Mary kind of person in a Martha kind of world, which of course refers to the event in the New Testament when Martha, exhausted from helping, came to Jesus and said,

"Lord, don't you care that my sister has left me to do the work by myself? Tell her to help me!"

"Martha, Martha," the Lord answered, "you are worried and upset about many things, but only one thing is needed. Mary has chosen what is better, and it will not be taken away from her."

Mary had chosen to sit at the feet of Jesus and listen rather than help with the chores.

Laura often complained in her newspaper columns that she felt "rushed" and "pushed about" by her many duties. As the more educated of the Almanzo and Laura husband-wife team, Laura took care of their farm accounting books, the home canning duties, the gardening enterprise, and the egg laying operation—for which she was widely known throughout the state of Missouri. As was true with many of his generation, Almanzo had only a few years of formal schooling.

Also, Laura was a joiner and doer in a myriad of good works for the community, holding office in the Masonic Eastern Star, being secretary-treasurer of the National Farm Loan Association, and serving with the Methodist Ladies Aid Society, among many other social activities. The harried homemaker complained that the motorcar did her little good because the new device only caused her to start late to a meeting, arrive after the program had started, and make her late getting home to fix supper for the "man of the place."

The fact is that Laura's volunteer involvement with the Eastern Star made it possible for her to do even more good works, but under a different banner. Yet Laura's need to feel useful warred with the more thoughtful, spiritual side of her personality. She even had vivid nightmares on the subject:

It had been a busy day and I was very tired, when just as I was dropping off to sleep I remembered that bit of mending I should have done for the man of the place. Then I must have dreamed, for in my fancy, I saw that rent in the garment enlarge and stretch into startlingly large proportions.

At the same time a familiar voice sounded in my ear, "A stitch in time saves nine," it said.

I felt very discouraged indeed at the size of the task before me and very much annoyed that my neglect should have caused it to increase to nine times its original size, when on the other side of me a cheerful voice insinuated, "It is never too late to mend."

Ah! There was that dear old friend of my grandmother who used to encourage her to work until all hours of the night to keep the family clothes in order. I felt impelled to begin at once to mend that lengthened rent, but paused as a voice came to me from a dark corner saying, "A chain is no stronger than its weakest link."

"Shall a man put new wine into old bottles," chimed in another. Of course not, I thought, then why put new cloth—.

But now the voices seemed to come from all about me. They appeared to be disputing and quarreling, or at least disagreeing among themselves. . . .

Now a couple of voices made themselves heard, evidently continuing a discussion.

"A rolling stone gathers no moss," said a rather disagreeable voice and I caught a shadowy glimpse of a hoary old proverb with a long, gray beard.

"But a setting hen never grows fat," retorted his companion in a sprightly tone.

"An honest man is the noblest work of God," came a high, nasal voice with a self righteous undertone.

"Ah, yes! Honesty is the best policy, you know," came the answer in a brisk business-like tone, just a little cutting.

"A fool and his money are soon parted," said a thin, tight-lipped voice with a puckering quality, I felt sure would draw the purse strings tight. . . .

But now there seemed to be danger of a really violent altercation for I heard the words "sowing wild oats," spoken in a cold, sneering tone, while an angry voice retorted hotly, "There is no fool like an old fool," and an admonitory voice added, "It is never too late to mend." Ah! Grandmother's old friend with a different meaning in the words.

Then at my very elbow spoken for my benefit alone, I heard again the words, "It is never too late to mend." Again I had a glimpse of that neglected garment with the rent in it grown to unbelievable size. Must I? At that time of night! But a soft voice whispered in my ear, "Sufficient unto the day is the evil thereof," [Matthew 6:34] and with a smile at grandmother's friend, I drifted into dreamless sleep.

One can almost feel what has been called "the tyranny of the urgent" disturbing her sleep.

But if life was sometimes a clamor of discordant voices for Laura, she also took great comfort in times of quiet reflection. The Mary side of her personality came out in a 1921 article in which she extolled a less traveled way to town. Laura concluded in this column that the way to peace and contentment had to be struggled for just as much as any other worthy goal. One didn't slide one's way downhill to peace but had to take varying paths that did not always lead in straight lines. Sometimes a person might have to backtrack to find the way to a better place of view. Nor was the journey boring. Just as one encountered the wonders of the babbling stream in going to town and resting under the branches of a sheltering hickory, nature, as created by God, could give rest along the way as well as at the end of the road.

The beauty of God's creation always inspired her. Her windows never had any curtains, and she trained turtles to come to her back door for a feeding. It was even something of a trial to have so much housework to do since she enjoyed helping Almanzo so much in the barn and in cutting wood.

But life was pretty much uphill most of the time, and the fact that there were obstacles along the way made the outcome of the journey all the more satisfying "when, after the effort of climbing, one reaches the hilltop there is a view of forest and fields and farmsteads and a wonderful skyscape for miles and miles, while on the slope at one's feet, the town is spread." It is at such times that joy comes to a person, and we become almost "light-footed" in our happiness as we have renewed energy to get back to work!

So which approach to life—the listening Mary or the preoccupied

Martha—won out in Laura? Frankly, it's hard to give a definitive answer. She continued to make resolutions in her columns to the effect that she was going to take time to enjoy life, as her grandparents are portrayed as doing in *Little House in the Big Woods,* chapters 7 and 8, but her neighbors in the Ozarks offered mixed views as to whether she achieved her resolutions or not.

"She's her husband's partner in every sense and is fully capable of managing the farm," one biographical sketch said. And a neighbor reported, "She gets eggs in the winter when none of her neighbors gets them." It takes *work* to get eggs in winter. One cannot idly gaze at the hens and watch them produce.

Parental and Church Influences

As much as Laura loved her pa, her mother was a stronger influence. She spent more time at her mother's knee than outdoors with him, even though he enlisted Laura's help when he could. Ma was always busy and very much like a Martha. Pa might play the fiddle after a long day and perhaps even relax a little by telling stories about his girls' aunts and uncles, but Ma was always beside him. While he sang and told stories, even then she kept on with her sewing into the evening darkness. "A woman's work is never done," an old proverb says, and Laura demonstrated how this is true in her chapter "The Whirl of Gaiety" from *Little Town on the Prairie.*

We are not told in the chapter whose idea it was to have a supper. No doubt the idea was bandied about by both men and women, but when it was decided to pay for the building of a church rather than to continue meeting at the railroad depot, there was no doubt as to who would cook the supper to raise the needed money!

Mrs. Wilder recounted—and one trusts her memory here, for she was involved—the many preparations and chores. She had to rush home from school to help her mother peel, slice, and stew a prodigious amount of pumpkin for pumpkin pies. She also gathered a quart of beans for a milk pan full of baked beans to be carried off to the evening's festivities. People ate voraciously, especially the men, it being for a good cause and all that. The women who were serving ate last, of course. In addition to roast pig, there were

heaped dishes of mashed potatoes and of mashed turnips, and of mashed yellow squash, all dribbling melted butter down their sides from little hollows in their peaks. There were large bowls of dried corn, soaked soft again and cooked with cream. There were plates piled high with golden squares of corn bread and slices of white bread and of brown, nutty-tasting graham bread. There were cucumber pickles and beet pickles and green tomato pickles, and glass bowls on tall glass stems were full of red tomato preserves and wild-chokecherry jelly. On each table was a long, wide, deep pan of chicken pie, with steam rising through the slits in its flaky crust.

It was a long evening for Laura and the others. While people were going back for second and third servings, the women were clearing away plates and washing them only to return them for further service. Supposedly, there was food set aside for the servers, but by the time it was their turn to eat, they were so tired the edge was gone off their appetites.

Later, when all the cleanup was done and the family returned home, Pa thanked Ma for her work at the Aid Society sociable, but Ma was still irritated by the heavy labor and made a remark that showed her exasperation. "It wasn't a sociable," she told Pa. "It was a New England Supper." Ma's remark about the New England Supper was one of the few times in her books that Laura allowed her mother to show anger to her spouse.

I believe the Martha side of Laura came from Ma, and with it the anger too. Many years later in a *Ruralist* column, Mrs. Wilder remarked rather bitterly about the way women were always being called "auxiliaries" to organizations when they had just as much right to be full members as the men did. Men alone didn't make communities; whole families did.

Of course, churches were still having suppers many years later. I enjoyed them tremendously, but then, as a boy, I never thought much about who did the work. I just knew that local gossip seemed more sanctified when the pumpkin pie was served by pious hands.

There is sadness about all this. Pioneer women were put on a pedestal, but they could be easily knocked off. Women were special enforcers of the moral code. Pa remarks in *Little Town on the Prairie* that women were an irresistible force when it came to reining in the evils of the saloon trade. The name Women's Christian Temperance Union speaks for itself. Yet as equal partners with their men in establishing the homestead, they had to get their hands dirty and do men's work too.

They could and did show that they could lead, own homesteads of their own, and run businesses—and do the household chores. But they didn't receive much credit for it, at least not politically. The struggle was wearying and the status not so high after all, and a single moral slip would knock them off that hard-won pedestal. The demands on women emerging from the shadows were overwhelming.

Laura observed all this over the years and even believed, in a way, that women should be not only home keepers but also moral examples and equal partners with men in running political affairs. But in an April 1919 article titled "Who'll Do the Women's Work?" she reflected on the aftermath of World War I:

Flaring headlines in the papers, have announced that "women will fight to hold jobs," meaning the men's jobs which they took when the men went to war. . . .

It makes our hearts thrill and our head rise proudly to think that women were found capable and eager to do such important work in the crisis of wartime days. I think that never again will anyone have the courage to say that women could not run world affairs if necessary. . . .

But this too is certain. We must advance logically, in order and all together if the ground gained is to be held. If what has hitherto been woman's work, in the world, is simply left undone by them, there is no one else to take it up. If in their haste to do other, perhaps more showy things, their old and special work is neglected and only half done, there will be something seriously wrong with the world, for the commonplace, home work of women is the very foundation upon which everything else rests.

So if we wish to go more into world affairs, to have the time to work at public work, we must arrange our old duties in some way so that it will be possible. . . .

We would like to keep up, if anyone can keep up with these whirling times and we must have more leisure from the treadmill if we are to do any of these things.

Yes, here is Laura's struggle in a nutshell: to balance the Mary and the Martha in her. As a pioneer, she was subject to the great expectations and the opportunities placed before the women of her day, but she also felt conflicted by a desire to pause and reflect on the glories of nature that God put around her. Yet such times could seem like the wasting of time with all that work waiting.

Laura quoted a typical Vermont housewife as saying to her hired girl, "Liza! Liza! Hurry up and come down! Today is wash day and the washing not started; tomorrow is ironing day and the ironing not begun; and the next day is Wednesday and here's the week half gone and nothing done yet."

Come to think of it, this Mary-versus-Martha struggle may apply to everybody. Right now, I'm feeling a little like mowing the lawn, cutting the hedge, trimming the grass along the edges of the sidewalk, replacing some dead flowers in the front yard, cultivating the back garden, and felling a few ugly hackberry trees. Of course, lying down in the hammock under the oak tree and meditating in a horizontal position sounds good too.

Maybe that Mary-and-Martha mix applies to us all.

Laura and Rose

The pioneers weren't psalm-singers . . . ; they believed in
God; they kept their powder dry, and prayed later. . . .
Courage isn't a matter of religion; it's a matter of character. And human courage has always been adequate to the
demands made upon it.

—ROSE WILDER LANE

Nineteen ninety-three was a landmark year in Laura Ingalls
Wilder scholarship because *The Ghost in the Little House*
by Dr. William Holtz, professor of English literature at the University
of Missouri, was published. It is a biography of Rose Wilder Lane. This
book revealed that Rose, a noted fiction writer and burgeoning political
thinker, had donated considerable amounts of her professional time and
talents to improving and even rewriting the famous Little House series.
The collaboration began when she lived with Laura and Almanzo in
the late 1920s and didn't end until the final book was done. Indeed, Dr.
Holtz credited much of the polish and smooth narrative development
of the series to Rose's professionalism and experience.

Because of these new insights into the Little House books, Rose's quotation, which begins this chapter, deserves special note. She was in the process of changing her whole political philosophy around the time she made these remarks in 1933, and they reveal how different her view of faith was from that of her mother. Dr. Holtz noted that later in her life Rose was an active participant at King Street Christian Church in Danbury, Connecticut, but it was hard to know what she believed. So daughter Rose may eventually have been something of a religious person, but she wasn't for much of her life and certainly not in the pioneer tradition of her mother.

In fact, it is possible that Rose may have tried to downplay her mother's faith in the Little House books. For example, in Laura's original *Pioneer Girl* manuscript she spoke several times about asking for forgiveness for wrongdoing. But this act of contrition did not show up as many times in the Little House series. However, admittedly, that subtle difference may provide scant actual proof.

What is more certain is that Rose, as a daughter and editor and rewriter of her mother's work, praised the virtues of self-reliance and hardy individuality over other qualities in the pioneers. In many ways, to Rose, man really was the "master of his fate." Humans were the measure of all things, while nature, at best, was indifferent to man and didn't tell him anything about man, let alone testify to the glory of God (see Psalm 19:1).

A Classic Series Is Wrought in Spite of Difficulties

Hence, mother and daughter had to grope their way forward to a mutual story line for the Little House series, with the cooperation not always being easy. One of my contacts in Mansfield told me that with

Laura and Rose, "blood was thicker than water." But both women did some bleeding before the work on the books was finished.

Practically all fans and scholars of Laura and Rose agree they shared similar personalities. And I agree as well. Both of them truly liked getting their own way, sometimes to the point of obsession.

For Mama Bess, getting her own way might have meant using manipulative tears to persuade Almanzo that he really *did want* to finish the twenty-eight-foot chimney for their fireplace, built with rocks gathered at the farm itself! This would not have been easy work for Almanzo, partially handicapped and standing at only five foot six. But Laura got her way, and the chimney to this day is a beautiful thing to behold as it climbs the side of their Rocky Ridge house a mile outside of Mansfield, near the Laura Ingalls Wilder Historic Home and Museum.

A neighbor once remarked to Laura that she always seemed to know how to get what she wanted, and Laura readily admitted that this was so. She was a leader and probably had the proverbial type A personality. Good leaders know how to get their way, and this also may be how they determine they are good leaders!

For all practical purposes, it was Laura who chose the very land the family was going to call their own, right near the town, when they first arrived in 1894. Yes, there was always a discussion with Almanzo before they moved ahead—on what Laura had already planned to do anyway.

The land that came to be named Rocky Ridge fits its name and sits on a hilltop overlooking a lot of land that would have been easier to farm. When the Wilders arrived, only about five of the forty acres had been improved—the rest was woods and brush. Even today anyone examining the place must wonder what kind of farmland Almanzo would have chosen if it had been his choice alone. Surely, the ground would have been flatter. Rocky Ridge deserved its name, as they picked up rock off the farm for years before Almanzo could really turn the soil or raise crops on it.

Fortunately for the man of the place, a previous settler had laid by those apple seedlings referred to earlier, and Almanzo used those trees as a start on making the farm pay. Although apple trees could take about seven years to bear fruit, the land immediately produced a wood crop for several years. Laura learned to use and then became proficient in using a crosscut saw for harvesting lumber. After some land was cleared, a small grain crop could be raised. Odd jobs, however, had to be Almanzo's lifeblood in the short term.

Mrs. Wilder was a helper, but she was also chief director. Mama Bess didn't even leave the preparation of the house's foundation to Almanzo but instead kept insisting that new carpenters be tried until a good one was found who would lay a foundation to *her* satisfaction. Since the house is still firmly standing, she must have been right!

The fact is, this tendency to lead or be in control is not something Laura ever hid. In *These Happy Golden Years,* the last book of the original Little House series, eighteen-year-old Laura makes it clear to Almanzo, twenty-eight, that although she loves him, she is uncomfortable with using the customary word *obey* in the marriage ceremony. She doesn't want to make a pretense or be untruthful or agree that a man is always right just because he is a man. Almanzo willingly agrees, as does Reverend Brown, but her stipulation was hardly typical of teenage girls of the 1880s.

Still, Laura learned, if she did not know it then, that total control over our lives is denied to us all. In Rose, she produced a daughter every bit as strong willed as she. Although the love between them was strong and abiding, at times they rubbed each other raw and went off in different directions.

For Rose, life was not a garden and her childhood was not a happy one according to many biographers. Right from the start, she found herself at odds with the town school. As a country child, she felt she was a poor and shabby specimen beside the town girls, who wore store-bought clothes. It didn't help much that she rode to school on a donkey, which was an embarrassment itself. Also, in her estimation the teachers were boring and, what was worse, stupid, according to her way of thinking.

Personally, I doubt any school or teacher could have pleased Rose when she was already so superior to other children in her intellectual prowess. She had an eye for facts and stuck to her guns when teachers were careless with them. She always won the school spelling bees. Standing out as a scholar only made her more isolated from others who sought popularity over academic achievement. It seems she eventually began skipping school to study at home, borrowing heavily from a neighbor's library to make up for the lack of class time.

Yet how difficult was her childhood really? Rose always could tell a good tale of woe and often did in diaries she later kept. She was undoubtedly fortunate to have had the parents she did. Few others of that time and place would have put up with her rebellious antics, which were those of a gifted, frustrated child. One thing I can't and won't believe is that Laura deliberately neglected her daughter, though some scholars have suggested it.

What Have I Raised?

One thing is clear: Laura was beside herself over what to do as Rose matured into her high school years. Then help came from startling quarters: Eliza Jane Wilder Thayer—the "lazy, lousy, Lizy Jane" of Laura's own not-always-obedient youth—offered to take Rose on.

This was none other than Almanzo's "bossy" sister from down south. Of the circumstances we know little. Had Laura and Eliza Jane somehow reconciled? There is just no family record. It is possible that Laura was beginning to realize she could no longer control her adventurous and now sexually curious daughter. So Rose was sent to live with her aunt Lizy Jane in Crowley, Louisiana, where she would attend high school.

The move to Crowley must have been liberating for Rose, but it didn't last long as she finished her only year of high school at the top of her class, cramming four years of Latin into one, among other academic achievements. She also had time for a beau, her first. Rose had a lively mind that quickly absorbed new ideas, and she was on her way as a "bachelor girl." No way would she become a farmer's wife; she would have a career. All these developments certainly must have fueled, not diminished, her mother's worries. The strong egos of both women didn't always make for easy going, either then or later on when work on the Little House series began. The fact that they were not religiously close did not help. In any case, in just a few years Rose learned telegraphy, married real estate salesman Gillette Lane, and settled in San Francisco, where opportunities seemed boundless at the turn of the twentieth century. Although a number of business ventures with Gillette had already revealed weaknesses in his abilities and in their marriage, the City by the Bay brought new promise. Rose and Gillette thought they'd make their fortune in California.

What Laura, with a more traditional morality and lifestyle, felt about all these ventures can only be understood indirectly from what she revealed in her writing for magazines and newspapers. On the one hand, she made it clear that she did not approve of young girls abandoning their role as home keepers, according to a *McCall's* article from

1919. On the other, she was happy for their liberation into new horizons too. No longer did unmarried women have to be considered just old maids, but new freedom didn't necessarily strengthen the home either. Laura had to learn to live with this dilemma herself, an idea she reflected in a 1918 *Ruralist* article:

> There were old maids when I was a girl. Later some of the older girls protested against being called old maids and insisted on being called "bachelor girls." There was some controversy over the question. . . . [But] I lost sight of it and awakened later to the fact that both old maids and bachelor girls had disappeared. . . . In their place are simply women, young women, older women . . . and widows, with the descriptive adjective in the background, but nowhere in the world, I think, are there any old maids.
>
> As one considers the subject, it becomes plain that this one fact contains the whole story and explanation of the change in the world for women. . . . In the days when old maids flourished, the one important fact in a woman's life was whether or not she were married and as soon as a girl child reached maturity she was placed in one of two classes and labeled accordingly.

There is every indication that as Laura saw her daughter embark on a writing career at the *San Francisco Bulletin,* she found inspiration to undertake a similar career of her own. But did she approve of some of Rose's more unconventional friends? On that she was silent. The agnosticism of some of them might have been a problem; still, she was beginning to follow the path of her daughter—one pioneer following in the steps of another pioneer.

Roles Are Reversed

A visit to Rose in 1915 found Laura eager to learn from her daughter-mentor the secrets of how to construct articles for the big national publications as a way of adding to the farm income. The money was needed. Whatever payments she was then receiving from the *Ruralist* would have been insignificant, maybe five to ten dollars per column at most, though her production for that paper increased dramatically in 1916.

Rose's earliest fiction appeared in serial form in the *San Francisco Bulletin* and was predictable, down to the happy endings for its aspiring protagonists. She wrote for the women's page of the paper, and the stories were rather pedestrian and even simplistic by today's standards. William Holtz has called the work "shamelessly clichéd romances."

It is not surprising, then, that mother and daughter collaborated on a series of poems for children while they were feeling their way toward better writing. Laura's efforts later appeared in the book *Laura Ingalls Wilder's Fairy Poems,* but this effort by Rose comes from the *Bulletin* itself.

> Under the stone that lies flat and brown,
> Down in the path by the garden wall,
> There is a city built upside-down,
> Houses, and gardens, and parks and all. . . .
>
> There live the Ant-People, in the dark,
> Bringing the little Ant-Babies up;
> Ant-Nurses carry them in the park,
> When they are good they have honey to sup.

High in the grass-tops the Ant-Cows roam,
Ant-Papas watch them with care lest they fall,
Milk them of honey, at night herd them home,
Bedding them safe in the Ant-Cows' stall.

Rose's superiorities as a writer have often been proclaimed, but it is good to know that both women had to grow from rather humble beginnings. Rose's reputation for skill and for meeting tight deadlines developed early in her career and allowed her to actually make a living as a writer, something that was hard to do then and hard to do today. Laura's recognition as a storyteller came later and only with the publication of her Little House series, beginning when she was sixty-five.

The historical record for the development of the children's series is well recorded, yet each account varies as to who should get credit for what it is that makes the stories shine as no other stories about the settling of the West do. I maintain that it is the stamp of the mother's religious beliefs; her philosophy, along with Henry Wadsworth Longfellow, that "homekeeping hearts are happiest"; and her sharp eye for domestic detail that are the crucial ingredients in the genius of the Little House books. Whatever struggles Laura and Rose may have gone through as mother and daughter, when it comes to the children's books themselves, it is the mother's story and not the daughter's editing that has counted for making them memorable and loved.

And whatever else they are, Laura's books are a story about building a *home* in the wilderness; they are not about raw nature itself, however raw that nature can be. No, the Christian family values of the books are overwhelming. The sacredness of home and hearth are everywhere present.

By contrast, Rose's growing view was that America is a land of self-made heroes. She expressed this first in *Let the Hurricane Roar,* but that is by no means the only place she expressed her belief in individualism as the highest philosophy. Dr. Holtz has pointed out that practically the whole of the Independence Day celebration described in *Little Town on the Prairie* is Rose's contrivance. There at the Fourth of July event, a budding politician raises his voice to praise "the glorious Fourth." America had done right to cast off a tyrannical power like Great Britain that had murdered women and children and encouraged Indian attacks on the defenseless.

The speaker goes on to tell of brave deeds done in Mexico and of opposition to tyrants who might be tempted to take advantage of a young country. But his main theme is that true Americans have always been self-reliant and have never needed help from anyone. We are a virtuous people who have pulled ourselves up by our own bootstraps.

While the Stars and Stripes flutters in the breeze, the Declaration of Independence is read aloud. A young Laura and Carrie had supposedly learned it by heart. And at the end of the reading, they feel like saying "Amen."

Then, perhaps as a result of Rose's influence, Laura wrote that Pa starts to sing "My Country, 'Tis of Thee" and others join in. After the song, Laura seems to have a moment of enlightenment when she concludes, "Americans won't obey any king on earth. Americans are free. That means they have to obey their own consciences." Then there is another paragraph that strays into the area of natural law and its meaning for Americans.

According to Dr. Holtz, these ideas represent Rose's newfound and burgeoning political philosophy and are not part of what Laura originally wrote. Of course, I do not think the strong-willed Laura would have been bowled over by her daughter—she must have thought in some way along these lines or wouldn't have approved the changes. Both of them were conservative women, and Laura would have especially agreed with the sentence that reads, "God is America's king."

What Is True Pioneering?

How different Laura's pioneers are from those of Rose when Laura is in control of her own narrative! Her family—though often isolated and struggling to find affordable land—still reached out to fellow settlers, which I would describe as following the admonition of Jesus to serve him by helping "the least of these." In one instance, in *By the Shores of Silver Lake,* the family puts a light in their window to guide folk lost along an unmarked trail (a historical fact, by the way). Laura's heroes were those who shared their goods with others, fellow pioneers journeying toward *mutual* fellowship and prosperity. For a settler can prosper and also hope that his neighbor prospers too.

Laura's prairie also taught lessons about a personal God—not just an abstract force but an ever-present Spirit, "a rock in a weary land, a shelter in the time of storm." As for the mysteries of human suffering, great life lessons could be learned at the hands of inevitable sorrow. No impersonal deity had forced them onto the prairie; they had chosen the risk for themselves, but they still needed his comfort and aid, for the task of pioneering was too big without him.

In a touching passage recorded in *Little Town on the Prairie,* Laura showed how her own faith in God had grown because of her sister Mary's struggle with blindness:

> Mary had always been good. Sometimes she had been so good
> that Laura could hardly bear it. But now she seemed different. . . .

"You used to try all the time to be good," Laura said. "And you always were good. It made me so mad sometimes, I wanted to slap you. But now you are good without even trying." . . .

"I'm not really [good]," Mary told her. "I do try, but if you could see how rebellious and mean I feel sometimes, if you could see what I really am, inside, you wouldn't want to be like me."

"I *can* see what you're like inside," Laura contradicted. "It shows all the time. You're always perfectly patient and never the least bit mean."

"I know why you wanted to slap me," Mary said. "It was because I was showing off. I wasn't really wanting to be good. I was showing off to myself, what a good little girl I was, and being vain and proud, and I deserved to be slapped for it."

Laura was shocked. Then suddenly she felt that she had known that, all the time. But, nevertheless, it was not true of Mary. She said, "Oh no, you're not like that, not really. You *are* good."

"We are all desperately wicked and inclined to evil as the sparks fly upwards," said Mary, using the Bible words. "But that doesn't matter."

"What!" cried Laura. . . .

"I don't know how to say what I mean very well. But—it isn't so much thinking, as—as just knowing. Just being sure of the goodness of God."

Laura stood still. . . . There Mary stood in the midst of the green and flowery miles of grass rippling in the wind, under the great blue sky and white clouds sailing, and she could not see. Everyone knows that God is good. But it seemed to Laura then that Mary must be sure of it in some special way.

I feel sure these reflections were genuine, right from Laura's heart. The greatness and goodness of God—how Laura dwelled on this theme in all her writing! In her columns and in her books, she returned time and again to Bible-informed perspectives.

In a November 1923 column she observed,

It seems to be instinctive for the human race to give thanks for benefits bestowed by a Higher Power. . . . A beneficent providence . . . has given us the harvest as well as countless other blessings thru the year. This is just another touch of nature that makes the whole world kin and links the present with the far distant past.

Mankind is not following a blind trail. . . . Let us, with humble hearts, give thanks for the revelation [given] to us and our better understanding of the greatness and goodness of God.

In another column, she remarked that the greatness and goodness of God could even be found in everyday chores, for "to sweep a room as to God's laws, makes that, and the action fine." This is a notion that almost seems quaint in our own times when so much religious writing emphasizes biblical principles that reveal "what's in it for me?" and so little is said about following and serving and washing each other's feet.

In another article, written in January 1919 when she was almost fifty-two years old—an age by which most people are well established in their views about faith matters—Laura revealed her spiritual sensitivity in her regret about possibly offending another woman. I maintain that her attitude revealed here—as well as her willingness to state this in a public forum—is strong evidence of a godly person responding to the nudges of the Spirit:

Mrs. G and I were in a group of women at a social affair, but
having a little business to talk over, we stepped into another
room where we were almost immediately followed by an
acquaintance. We greeted her and then went on with our
conversation, from which she was excluded. I forgot her
presence and when I looked her way again she was gone. We
had not been kind and, to make it worse, she was compara-
tively a stranger among us.

In a few minutes every one was leaving, without my having
had a chance to make amends in any way. I could not apologize
without giving a point to the rudeness. . . . Now I learn that it
will be months before I see her again. I know that she is very
sensitive and that I must have hurt her. Again and from the
bottom of my heart, I prayed "The Fool's Prayer,"

These clumsy feet, still in the mire,
Go crushing blossoms without end;
These hard, well-meaning hands we thrust
Among the heart-strings of a friend.
O Lord, be merciful to me, a fool.

As we grow old enough to have a proper perspective, we see
such things work out to their conclusion. . . . Very few of our
misdeeds are with deliberate intent to do wrong. Our hearts are
mostly in the right place but we seem to be weak in the head.

For Laura, even animals taught spiritual things. Her pet in the
Little House series, Jack the bulldog, provided a constant example of
faithfulness and courage. This is so much the case that when Jack fi-

nally dies, Laura hopes he will find a place with her in the afterlife. Pa assures her that there must be "Happy Hunting Grounds" for dogs like Jack. Laura continued to have a lifelong love of animals and attributed spiritual qualities to her dogs: the attribute of apology to one dog, who offered his paw after having mistaken a friend for a stranger, and to another dog, who was blind, the quality of wondering, *Why me?*

The God and Father of Us All

Laura believed there was a vital life connection between the temporal and the eternal. All truth, whether in nature or in Scripture, was God's truth—and that truth remained basically the same from generation to generation. When the value of Christianity was questioned after the carnage of World War I, Laura defended her faith in a December 1919 *Ruralist* article: "Here and there one sees a criticism of Christianity because of the things that have happened and are still going on. 'Christian civilization is a failure,' some say. 'Christianity has not prevented these things, therefore it is a failure,' say others."

But Laura went on to maintain that true Christianity among the nations hadn't been tried at all. Christianity was known about but wasn't practiced because it had been found difficult. People should have followed through with what Christ taught rather than give up at the first challenge brought on by the Great War.

She also noted that if we are going to fail in applying true Christian teaching to our own lives, we cannot expect to see it appear from a lawless mob, which is exactly what we are doing when we fail in our individual Christian responsibilities. Therefore, Laura insisted that we should "do the right thing always." Just as individuals make up the whole of a nation's culture, so do individual actions make up the moral fiber of society. In other words, do good, and that act will come back to bless you in ways you did not expect.

In her *Ruralist* column from June 1918 she praised a local attorney for living out the golden rule by not taking a case because he knew doing so would do irreparable harm to two neighbors. He showed that honesty is not just the best policy; it is the only policy and bears real consequences for good. The attorney in her story ended up with another case on the recommendation of the client he had persuaded not to bring suit. "Cast thy bread upon the waters: for thou shalt find it after many days," says Ecclesiastes 11:1. "If there were a cry of 'stop thief!' we would all stand still," Laura said in this same *Ruralist* column. Yet she maintained that there is still hope that we will do the right thing because Christian teaching permeates society.

In another column, Laura reflected on an argument among neighbors and saw the truth of Proverbs 15:1 lived out: "A soft answer turneth away wrath." The wrath was turned away by the kind answers of the one toward whom the anger was directed. Having prepared for a fight, the angry party was left with nothing to say and a foolish look on her face. Mrs. Wilder commented that the angry woman "might as well have tried to break a feather pillow by beating [it]" as to start an argument in the first place. She went on to say,

> Until this incident, I had found no more in the words than the
> idea that a soft answer might cool the wrath of an aggressor, but
> I saw wrath turned away as an arrow deflected from its mark
> and come to understand that a soft answer and a courteous
> manner are an actual protection.

In Laura I see a more traditional Christian ethic that says the old values being expressed—shown to us by father and mother, family and the church—are the values that can carry us forward into the future.

Rose, the Less Traditional

Yet how different were Rose's views on the influence of religion, especially as it related to America's essential beliefs and direction forward. In a March 2, 1933, article for the *Mansfield Mirror* newspaper, Rose wrote,

> The symbols and even the essentials of religious belief vary from country to country and age to age while the fundamental struggle of human life against the *lifeless universe* [italics added] is always and everywhere the same. I wasn't dealing with religious belief but with the more elemental struggle when I wrote about Caroline and Charles [in *Let the Hurricane Roar*]. And so, in fact, were the American pioneers when they went west.
>
> The pioneers weren't psalm-singers or quarrelers about creeds. . . . Don't forget that a greater part of the pioneer advance was made by Quakers and by Unitarians and Congregationalists, all of which dispensed as much as possible with religious creeds and forms. Courage isn't a matter of religion; it's a matter of character. *And human courage has always been adequate to the demands made upon it* [italics added]. Our very existence today is proof of that.

A writer expressing these views today would be labeled, more than likely, a secularist. Such sentiments are if anything more mainstream now than a more traditional view that places God at the center of existence. In post–World War I America, however, Rose's viewpoint would have been considered at best a minority view and at worst heretical.

In contrast to Rose, Laura viewed the influence of the Christian faith as essential and not marginal. While she would not have denied that courage is a valuable character trait, I don't believe she would have separated it from the influence of religious faith or maintained that the influence of religious faith on communities was insignificant. Yes, individuals could overlook doctrinal differences among Baptists, Presbyterians, Methodists, and Catholics—the main Christian groups that had settled the West (Unitarians and Quakers being too small in number to have had the influence Rose claimed). But religious conviction, or lack of it, shaped the whole culture of this country. Gallup polls have always shown Americans to be far more religious than other Western cultures. This was not the case without deliberate effort and evangelical intent, as Laura herself demonstrated by what she wrote.

Mama Bess Speaks Her Mind

The fact is, the importance of the influence of private faith on public morality became a theme of Mrs. Wilder's, especially during the moral crucible of World War I. An August 1918 column made a point that I'm confident was first taught to her at her mother's knee:

> I heard a boy swear the other day, and it gave me a distinctly
> different kind of a shock than usual. I had just been reading
> an article in which our soldiers were called crusaders who were
> offering themselves, in their youth as a sacrifice in order that
> right might prevail against wrong and that those ideals, which

are in effect the teachings of Christ, shall be accepted as the law
of nations.

When I heard the boy use the name of Christ in an oath,
I felt that he had belittled the mighty effort we are making,
and that he had put an affront upon our brave soldiers by
using lightly the name of the great Leader who first taught the
principles for which they are dying. The boy had not thought
of it in this way at all. He imagined that he was being very bold
and witty, quite a grown man in fact.

I wonder how things came to be so reversed from the right
order, that it should be thought daring and smart to swear,
instead of being regarded as utterly foolish and a sign of weak-
ness, betraying a lack of self-control. If people could only realize
how ridiculous they appear when they call down the wrath of
the Creator and Ruler of the Universe just because they have
jammed their thumbs. I feel sure they would never be guilty of
swearing again. It is so out of proportion, something as foolish
and wasteful as it would be to use the long-range gun which
bombarded Paris [Big Bertha], to shoot a fly. If we call upon the
Mightiest for trivial things, upon whom or what shall we call in
the great moments of life?

Catholic journalist G. K. Chesterton once wrote that "angels can
fly because they can take themselves lightly." Similarly, Laura found it
best to approach her own moral pretentions lightly, even as she preached
her religious views:

"You have so much tact and can get along with people so well,"
said a friend to me once. Then after a thoughtful pause she

added, "But I never could see any difference between tact and trickery." Upon my assuring her that there was no difference, she pursued the subject further.

"Now I have no tact whatever, but speak plainly," she said pridefully. "The Scotch people are, I think, the most tactful and the Scotch, you know, are the trickiest nation in the world."

As I am of Scotch descent, I could restrain my merriment no longer and when I recovered enough to say, "You are right, I am Scotch," she smiled ruefully and said, "I told you I had no tact."

Tact does for life just what lubricating oil does for machinery. It makes the wheels run smoothly and without it there is a great deal of friction and the possibility of a breakdown.

I sometimes wonder if Laura occasionally thought of her own daughter in light of this sentiment. Laura was going to need a good deal of tact in the difficult waltz that was their relationship, particularly in the years between 1928 and 1935, when they lived so close together that sometimes they worked out of the same house, a house that had been all Laura's until Rose resettled in Mansfield and moved in with her parents.

Those were heavy years of turmoil and fruitful labor.

Building the Little House

Just come and visit Rocky Ridge,
Please grant us our request;
We'll give you all a jolly time—
Welcome the coming; speed the parting guest.

—LAURA INGALLS WILDER

The reality is that Laura Ingalls Wilder was not a person who thought it necessary or appropriate to reveal her private thoughts on topics or people to the outside world. She certainly extended this attitude to her spirituality, which she definitely considered one of the most private of matters. As I mentioned earlier, Laura didn't like to hear people testify at prayer meeting on Wednesday nights. She said it "offended [her] sense of privacy." Hers was a quiet-voiced religion but not a silent one.

By contrast, Rose was much more direct in expressing her convictions, be they about politics, religion, or the right way to construct a book. Thus, I do wonder if Rose—who did not share much of Laura's Christian worldview—tempered some of Laura's faith material to shape it to her own liking. To better understand how and why this might have happened, it will be helpful to invest some attention into learning more about Rose and her views as an author.

The Writing Coach?

As a determined professional writer, Rose cherished a vision that her mother could become a professional writer as well. Rose loved Mama Bess but couldn't get her to take the writing counsel she wished to give. At least that was the way she felt when Laura produced—in her opinion—substandard work. After all, based on her vast amounts of publishing experience, Rose was the "expert" when it came to writing, and she was stridently unhappy at times about her mother's writing endeavors. Even though the *Missouri Ruralist* eventually grew to have a circulation of one hundred thousand readers, Laura's income of a few dollars per column wouldn't have gone far in financing the family. Rose felt that longer, connected narratives were necessary for writing success—not the short anecdotal articles, often ending with a moral, that Laura was penning for the *Ruralist*. But Mama Bess seemed oblivious to the advice, as well as to the money she could make from writing for the bigger markets, where a more secular view was clearly preferred and expected.

I think one can understand, given the poor nature of the soil at Rocky Ridge, why Rose's temper sometimes flared in frustration. The farm probably produced no more than a few hundred dollars of net profit per year. So when in 1919 Laura published a major article in *McCall's* magazine, Rose was quick to advise that writing, as a sideline, was the best way to make money for the family.

To be fair to Laura, I think she was actually trying to do the things Rose suggested but just couldn't so far as the writing instruction went. Her limited education was unequal to the task. Although she had taught three terms of school on the prairie, she also once admitted that she had never graduated from any school she ever attended. Permission to teach had come through a certificate, not through a degree.

Rose was making several hundred dollars per published piece in magazines such as *Sunset* and the *Saturday Evening Post* when she first moved back to Mansfield in 1924. Her O. Henry Award–winning short story, "Innocence," had earned her $1,500 alone. Although the bond between mother and daughter was not perfect, it was strong enough to draw them together for important literary work, however at odds they could be. The fact is that Rose had plenty of opportunity to stay away from Mama Bess and from the Ozarks, yet time and again she returned to her mother and to Mansfield to do her work and to contribute to the miracle of the Little House series. They eventually decided to work together for the higher cause of these books.

Fans of Laura's classics owe a great deal of gratitude to Dr. John E. Miller, professor emeritus of history at South Dakota State University, for his work outlining the ins and outs of Laura and Rose's working relationship in his book *Becoming Laura Ingalls Wilder*. He took pains to explain how Laura's simple ideas of a book commemorating some of Pa's stories became a connected saga of her adventurous family's life. He recorded how the series developed every step of the way and how Rose's role became ever bigger in the development as she took Laura's handwritten manuscripts and ran them through her typewriter to shape the narrative into what we now read.

Rose Reaffirms Homespun Values

Now I should like for Rose to speak her own mind about the changes in her thinking that allowed her to work with her mother. In an article of her own for the *Missouri Ruralist* in May 1925, Rose gave us the best insight we have into her developing acceptance of her mother as someone with whom she could work, with some reservations here and there.

Now I have come back to the farm.

And this is a joke on me. For it was 15 years ago, when I was still intoxicated with all that the city offers, that my parents were offered an opportunity for city life. The offer was a good one, meaning at once as much as the farm was giving them, and opening vistas that were positively glittering. [Researchers have no idea what this "opportunity" was.]

I was enthusiastic for the change. I was a newly grown-up daughter, and if that alone had not made me feel infinitely wiser than my parents, my city experience would have done so. They were dears, but they couldn't know as much as I did. I took their life in hand and splendidly made it over in every detail; I knew exactly what they should do and exactly how they should do it. The only difficulty with my plan was my parents. They wouldn't move. [Rose did manage to get her mother and father out of their house, but that was later. And it wasn't easy. Then she was able to take over the old homeplace, and for a while Laura and Almanzo lived in a nearby cottage!]

Driven by my fierce arguments to her last defense, my mother said: "I don't see why we should. Why should we move to a city and work 15 or 20 years to get money enough to retire to a farm? Because I notice that's what city people are always planning to do and working for. We already have the farm."

"That's different," I said impatiently. "City people don't mean ever to live on a farm. What they want is a country place."

"Well," my mother said mildly, "this farm is a country place. We can move to St. Louis and work hard 15 years or so, save our money then have a country place. Or we can stay here and keep on working hard, enjoying the country place as we go along and then have it. It comes to the same thing in the end." . . .

Success. The joys of creative work, the joys of its recognition. I have written my books. But my father and mother have made their farm; two hundred acres of good land, well fenced, productive.

They made it, with their hands and brains, from poor acres of thin hillside land, from washed gullies and sassafras patches. They built this house, with its sleeping porches and verandas, its big stone fireplace, its filled bookshelves, its white-enameled kitchen, its modern bathroom. This was a dream of theirs, realized thru creative labor, as my books are made. The reward of it to them is the same as mine to me.

So, as my mother said, it comes to the same thing in the end. Here I am, back on the farm, and finding here all the variety, the beauty and the human satisfactions that can be packed into my days.

Having left us with a sense that "east or west, home is best" and that rejuvenation could be found in the country, Rose promptly left the farm again in 1926 after only two years of chicken keeping and freelance writing to travel first to Paris and then to Albania with her friend Helen Boylston, writer of the Sue Barton nurse series. The Albanian adventure seems to have been a highlight for both women, and Rose always maintained that some prince or high official had proposed marriage to her, but the details are sketchy. The letters to Mama Bess were glowing, and yet she began to tell friends that she needed to return to Missouri. There was no necessary financial pressure to do so, yet she felt compelled to go. What I suspect is that for profound but unspecified emotional reasons, Rose needed Laura as much as Laura needed Rose. Laura was the star to which Rose's compass needle always pointed for approval.

The Loving Daughter

Although Rose's time in Albania remained a dear memory, the time there was brief. She returned to Rocky Ridge after only two years in Tirana, the capital of Albania, but something had changed. When she was really honest with herself, she realized she didn't want to be lost in the Ozarks again, but she did good work there and needed to keep working. Much material for her fiction writing came from her knowledge of the land and its people and of Laura and Almanzo's life.

Rose also felt a gnawing sense of responsibility for her parents—she was the protective hen to her little chicks. They must have seemed such hopeless innocents to their worldly daughter of forty-two. Their parochialism and narrow ways created an anxiety for her. They economized when they should be enjoying the fruits of their labor, and they associated with dull friends.

Fun Times at Rocky Ridge

In 1928, at a time when a forty-two-year-old child didn't do this, Rose (and her friend Helen Boylston) moved back into the old farmhouse, and they and Rose's parents all lived together, each doing their separate work. Laura was doing her part to help Almanzo run the farm while beginning to have thoughts about doing a reminiscence of her parents' lives. Rose was writing her articles. Helen was busy with her own projects. One does wonder what Laura and Almanzo thought about having these extra guests in such cramped quarters.

The whole assemblage was not without resources, though we don't quite know what the Wilders themselves felt about their finances. Personally, Rose concluded they needed "support" and proceeded to give it in spades. Making occasional gifts to them of five hundred dollars, she began to plan how to improve their standard of living—and her own.

Flush with cash from continued rises in the stock market, Rose proceeded to build a cottage for her mother and father, even as they protested that such a gift was too generous. They were perfectly happy in the old home, which they had built with their own hands from material right off their property. Role reversals are aggravating.

Nevertheless, Rose had her way and the cottage was built even as the Great Depression suddenly arrived and began to wipe out her savings. The house—first estimated at a cost of $2,000—gradually became an $11,000 English-style cottage. You can see it today at the Laura Ingalls Wilder Historic Home and Museum near Mansfield.

The truth is, Rose's energy was astonishing. While suffering much self-doubt about her own talents, she ghostwrote books for famous news broadcaster Lowell Thomas and finished *White Shadows in the South Seas* for Frederick O'Brien. She also had time to write, during a productive period from 1925 to 1928, *He Was a Man, Hill-Billy, Gordon Blake,* and *Cindy: A Romance of the Ozarks.*

All the more surprising considering all this productivity—moving in with her parents, starting a new house for her mom and dad, writing books of her own, and beginning to help her mother conceptualize what later became the Little House series—was Rose's emotional state.

We know from her diaries that she battled a lifelong war with depression, yet she could turn out an amazing amount of work, even during her darkest times. Often these times were not blue, as in "she had the blues." They were black. But from 1928 until she left the farm for good in 1935, she produced a best-selling novel, wrote numerous short stories for the *Saturday Evening Post* and other popular magazines, and most notably provided crucial editorial work on her mother's expanding series of books, the first of which was published in 1932.

Once again in touch with nature and the stimulation of wildness and woods, Rose's creative energy was restored by the natural piety such an environment brings. For Laura this effect had always been there. For Rose it was a come-and-go sort of thing. I believe that in the Little House series, some of the stunning details of the natural world and the vicissitudes of the weather are a result of Rose's celebrated gifts as a writer. What I am describing is revealed in another excerpt from Rose's *Ruralist* article:

> This morning was not yet light when I woke and stretched an arm out of coziness into the chill of my room. A glow of lamplight came up the back stairs into the hall outside my open door, and from the kitchen I heard my mother's steps going back and forth, the rattle of wood going into the cookstove, a clanking of milk pails, then the slam of the kitchen door. Nero, the Airedale pup, barked in circles around the milk pails as they went toward the barn. . . .
>
> The chimney from the dining-room heater comes up thru my bedroom and I dressed close to its warmth. The bathroom water heater is out of order, has been out of order for months while we send the leaky fittings back and forth between the

farm and plumber's shop in the city. Seems like you can't get
an honest job done anywhere, these days.

My mother had a basin of soft water warmed on the
stove for me when I went downstairs. It had been a cold night;
an edging of frost on the window panes was melting in the
warmth. . . .

This morning I left her to watch the breakfast while I
trudged to the henhouse with the pails. There is a warm, feathery
feeling in a henhouse. The feed steamed as I spooned it into the
troughs, and then hens came fluttering from their perches. . . .

"This is sheer egotism," I said to my feeling of happiness in
dispensing such complete happiness to those hundreds of hens.

I came back thru the barn alley. . . .

On one side of the alley are the box stalls, where Fanny and
Kate and gentle Governor, the Morgan stallion, had finished
their bran and were turning floury noses to their mangers. They
whickered greetings as I passed. On the other side are the cows.
My father, in his milking apron, was lifting a pail of milk to the
hanging scales. . . .

"That Jersey's the best little cow I ever raised," my father
said, transferring the scale's figures to the Jersey's record with a
carpenter's pencil. "If she don't give pretty nearly her weight of
milk in another 30 days I miss my guess."

There was deep satisfaction in his voice and eyes. It was the
indescribable feeling I have when I have written a story that is
the very best I can do; there was the sense of creation in it, and
the workman's joy in a good job done. . . .

"Yes sir, a darn good cow!" my father said, slapping her
flank, while she turned large eyes upon us in the lantern light,

and licked her nose. Nero whined for attention, and we looked down at his eagerness of uplifted paw. That exuberant pup is constrained by affection to obey our laws, but sometimes it's very hard for him. . . .

Outside the barn the morning was gray, and as I came up the path I was surprised to see my mother, wrapped in a shawl, standing outside the kitchen door. "Hurry!" she called to me. "It's changing every second!"

The barn behind me was black against a rosiness in the east, but it was not the sky she wished for me to see. It was the evanescent colors, the lights and shadows subtly changing down the length of the valley at the coming of the dawn. We stood and watched them silently till the rosy sky faded to the color of water, and sunshine came yellow across the fields. A new day was there, a day as miraculous and fresh as tho it were the first that ever dawned, and a chill little wind that ran before it went westward, followed by a promise of warmth.

A Family Classic Emerges from Troubled Waters

Rose left Rocky Ridge again in 1935. It had been a productive but emotionally unnerving stay, as times with her mother always were. She had written a strong bestseller in *Let the Hurricane Roar,* and she had helped Laura attain a degree of financial independence she had never known before. But Rose was weary of Mansfield itself.

Perhaps the main thing to remember is that these years together were incredibly productive for both women. The sunshine was out there too, peeking through and around whatever clouds dotted their skies, because this is the time during which Laura began, in consultation with Rose, to formulate her pioneer memoir.

In conducting interviews for my book *"I Remember Laura,"* I asked people (primarily in the Mansfield area) what may have prompted Mrs. Wilder to begin her books, despite her limitations as a writer. Many of them related variations of the same story: what had really inspired Mrs. Wilder to begin to reconstruct her past and record it for posterity was the concern that many of her memories and Pa's stories would be lost, and this just seemed a shame.

She wasn't saying she was the only living person to have pioneered, but somehow she had always felt that her own little family was special, perhaps given a God-ordained experience that had value to encourage others. Her only question to her nearby neighbors was what they thought about it. Did they feel other people would be interested in knowing about pioneer days? Her neighbors, according to the ones I interviewed, universally said yes, she should put her life down in writing. And, happily, Rose was by her side in the place she needed to be.

I believe an element of nostalgia for the past also played a part in Laura's decision at age sixty-three to become a late-blooming author of books. Her *Ruralist* columns, which she no longer wrote—she was reaching retirement age, after all—often painted somewhat rosy hues of long ago. Virtue, which she believed the country was losing, could be found way back there in the faith and modeling of mother and father. The distant past also showed that we had used more common sense back then. We didn't depend on the government's advice so much. We used our own brain to know how to polish our shoes or when to plant grain.

In many of Laura's articles, it is clear that many people taking up farming, at least in the Ozarks, were doing so experimentally, just getting advice from friends and then trying it out. Farm papers like the *Ruralist* were made for just such people. One gets the impression that what secrets Laura had learned about chickens had come from her own close observation of them.

One can almost feel Laura's sense of satisfaction in reporting to her Missouri readers that in days gone by, the plucky pioneers had learned to make lamps out of buttons, cloth, and grease, and that they had learned to grind grain by simply adapting the coffee mill for the needed purpose. Yes, yearning for the good old days when things were simpler and the good life was more elemental could exert an attractive pull.

All of her beloved little family were dead, save Carrie, who still lived in South Dakota near Mount Rushmore, and Grace, who still lived near De Smet. She missed them all terribly. The only time she had been able to go back to De Smet solely for family reasons had been for Pa's death in 1902.

To become reacquainted with the people she loved most meant she had to remember the scenes of her childhood, when faith and hope were bright and anything seemed possible. Were they times, as well, when the circumstances of life on the edge of the frontier required deeper attachment to the Almighty?

Rose also very much considered herself a pioneer and certainly the daughter of pioneers, a fact of which she was exceedingly proud. She, too, somehow felt that there was virtue to be found in mining the past, though she probably wasn't looking for any particular religious affirmations.

Rose's vision of the pioneer moving west included many examples of humans standing on their own to fulfill their destiny. More and more she had come to like the idea of the bold and courageous individual as a pinnacle of human development. The discovery of personal freedom was the great thing to extol.

But Rose wanted the facts. She would interpret them how she felt best, but she wanted the facts as much as Laura did. One of her great services to Laura was in being a stickler about getting the details right. She encouraged her mother in her research and queried Laura when she had her doubts about her mother's memory.

For example, was there really a crab in Plum Creek, when to Rose's knowledge all crabs were saltwater and found in the ocean?

Wouldn't it be better in *The Long Winter* to include the fact that another couple had been living with the family during those storied days and nights lasting from October to May?

Could Laura really remember anything from the Kansas prairie, when in fact she had been only two or three years old when Ma and Pa had pioneered there? Together and independently, mother and daughter did research on where Laura had lived in Kansas. Laura really thought at one point that it might have been near Fort Scott, when in fact that location would have been more than one hundred miles from where they had actually settled. The details needed to be right. So Laura and Rose took a drive to scout the territory. (Why didn't they just consult a map? I don't know.) On this trip they may have first learned about Dr. Tan (actually Tann), although more likely, Pa had told Laura about him. Dr. Tan was the black doctor who showed up to help the Ingallses recover from malaria in *Little House on the Prairie*.

I believe both women equally wanted the facts, but they had to negotiate what to do with them in the fictional books. Sometimes facts help a good story, and sometimes they don't.

It was Rose who realized early on that the Little House series, as a personal narrative seen through Laura's eyes, required that the young heroine be at least two years older than she really was to be a credible firsthand observer. This major editorial decision—a change in point of view to the narrative—cannot be minimized in its benefit to readers.

Another editorial contribution of Rose's is also crucial and may have been her most significant: where necessary, she filled out Laura's sometimes sparse story by adding arresting details that fleshed out the narrative. In *Little House on the Prairie* in just one brief paragraph, Rose displayed her genius. In the scene in chapter 5, Pa is building the little log home, and Rose had Laura note that as the sun shone through chinks in the logs, "everything was striped there. Stripes of sunshine came through the cracks in the west wall, and stripes of shadow came down from the poles overhead. The stripes of shade and sunshine were all across Laura's hands and her arms and her bare feet. And through the cracks between the logs she could see stripes of prairie."

Time after time, Rose aided Laura in this way with her writer's eye, and we fans of the series are forever indebted to her.

A Dynamic Writing Coalition

Given the facts of the case, as gathered from these and other sources, here's how I think Laura and Rose managed to make progress on the Little House series through the hectic years of the Depression, with all its financial strain. Their personality issues and the pressures of potential financial ruin would have brought on rather natural clashes and mis-understandings. But Laura, taking the raw material of her life, started out alone to shape a story that at first merely preserved the memories from her youth and Pa's familiar tales handed down to her. And many of these tales do turn up in just such a way in *Little House in the Big Woods*.

Then the vision of what the books could become grew from there because both women were creatively ambitious and in need of financial success. And they knew there was more to say than had been said in the first book. So there came a second book—about Almanzo's early boyhood in Malone, New York—and a third. And by then their vision for the series expanded into homage to all pioneers while still stressing family values, as Laura would have insisted, and self-reliance, as Rose would have insisted.

Rose—because of her background and greater experiences in the outside world—contributed to the big picture, to the larger issues of western settlement, and to the need for the individuals to make themselves into independent Americans. Laura guarded her domestic vision of hearth and home and Christian values that make community possible. God had to be in the Little House stories to fully account for Laura's experiences of him.

Because I think this view better fits with Laura's personality and with what the books come to mean to people who read them, independent of an understanding of Rose's political and philosophical input, I tend to side with those scholars such as Pamela Smith Hill, Dr. John E. Miller, and William Anderson who hold that Laura grew during the writing process and eventually made her books her own vision of the West rather than Rose's starker vision of a struggle against fate. However, Dr. William Holtz's view that Rose essentially rewrote the books can't be ruled out.

With such an effective and powerful editorial hand, and with Laura leaning on her expertise, did Rose also somewhat dilute the centrality of faith in the story of this pioneer family? Admittedly it is true that at many times during the composition of the Little House series the women found themselves disagreeing over substantial matters, but I find it was almost always Mama Bess who won in setting the tone for *her* story.

As to the heavy editing and rewriting that Rose did, Hill's case is strong that this was just standard editorial procedure, with which Rose would have had more experience. While there are a few people who turn in an almost perfect copy on their first attempts at a book, I've found from my own experience in working with publishing companies that this phenomenon rarely happens. It's a wonder to see how some writers get something into print without going through this major refining process, but few authors avoid multiple revisions.

Hill cited a letter Rose wrote to her mother in 1931 as evidence of a common editorial practice. Editor Marion Fiery of Knopf wanted substantial changes in what had been presented as a picture book. Fiery outright rejected the idea of a picture book and asked for an expanded narrative in the third person. Rose explained to her mother the reasoning behind this, saying, "'I' books do not sell well."

Rose, knowing how her mother would be overwhelmed by such a change, suggested that if Laura didn't feel up to writing the book from a third-person point of view, she could simply write in the first person and Rose would make the grammatical changes. Though Fiery was ultimately not able to work on the children's series, her suggestion led to a fully fleshed-out narrative extending over several volumes instead of a soon-to-be-forgotten series of picture books using childlike dialogue.

The point is, collaboration is the norm, not the exception, when it comes to books, and the Little House series simply followed the norm.

In the end, Laura and Rose survived the Depression and their collaboration. Thus, out of seeming disunity, a deeper unity evolved. The Little House series became not many voices but one voice—the voice of Pa's fiddle speaking peace to the wild winds of the prairie.

Songs in the Night

I picked a wild sunflower, and as I looked into its golden
heart, such a wave of homesickness came over me that I
almost wept. I wanted Mother, with her gentle voice and
quiet firmness; I longed to hear Father's jolly songs and to
see his twinkling blue eyes.

—LAURA INGALLS WILDER

We know that when Pa's fiddle sang it played many tunes of gaiety
and good cheer to the little family on the prairie. Family singing
was popular in the days before electricity made entertainment available
at the push of a button. Humorous tunes such as "The Arkansas Traveler," "Captain Jinks," and "Oh! Susanna" were very familiar to the
Ingallses through Pa's one-man musical band. The family's song collection contained an extensive number of tunes for mere enjoyment.

Yet undoubtedly the most impactful songs in Pa's repertoire were
the many hymns that the family—including Laura—sang together. In
the Little House series, Laura made it clear the many fun and entertain-
ing songs the family sang were not sufficient to sustain the family
through rugged days of prairie living, particularly during a hard winter.

The little family needed stronger stuff than mere melody to keep hope and faith alive as tough times kept coming the farther west they moved.

The fact is, Laura referred time and again to the many hymns and sacred songs that Pa played to strengthen the family in their various little homes. I count approximately thirty hymns that are either from hymnbooks or from what they'd learned from memory, lacking those books because of their cost. Even patriotic standards could be made into hymns to teach civic virtue, such as "Hail, Columbia" by Joseph Hopkinson:

> Hail Columbia, happy land!
> Hail, ye heroes, Heaven-born band!
> Firm, united let us be,
> Rallying 'round our liberty,
> As a band of brothers joined
> Peace and safety we shall find.

"Hail, Columbia" may not be particularly religious, but it was found in many hymnals of the day and did suggest there was a "future and a hope" for the brave who were making our country a "city upon a hill," as the governor of Massachusetts, John Winthrop, had said of the Massachusetts Bay Colony in his 1630 sermon "A Model of Christian Charity."

The Ingalls family and the Wilder brothers especially needed to believe there was a future and a hope laid out for them as they continually took on nature's raw edge in a new land. They were building on that first golden dream of the pilgrims. Nation building requires stirring words, long commitment, and stout hymns.

Both families would have been willing to settle for good in Minnesota—where the rainfall was slightly more regular than what was to be found near De Smet—but the grasshopper plagues of the late 1870s forced the Ingallses to keep moving farther into ever more troublesome territory, as it turned out. Even the more prosperous Almanzo, whose family was well off, went west too. He was looking for cheaper land than could be found near his father's farm in Spring Valley, Minnesota. None of the pioneers, young or old, ever quite knew what lay ahead. But, then, do we even now? The times may be different, but the challenges are still great.

Songs Give Vision to a Journey

The fact is, heaven and fellowship with the Almighty become more and more important as our hopes face the stern tests of life. We discover that the promise of a new sunrise may only presage the next storm beyond the horizon. So perhaps it is good to look at what songs of the faith did for the Ingalls family and also for Almanzo in order to better understand the consolations and encouragements of what are still called the songs of Zion, that city upon a hill.

Fortunately, we are greatly aided in our understanding of Laura's faith background by knowing the name of a hymnal that included many of the hymns that so greatly influenced her. *Pure Gold for the Sunday School* was first published in 1871 and is referred to familiarly by Carrie Ingalls in an August 1940 letter to Laura as the hymnal belonging to her and perhaps passed down by Pa and Ma. (Hymn 18 from *Pure Gold* is referred to in *Little Town on the Prairie*.)

Published by Biglow & Main, the hymnal was edited by Robert

Lowry and W. Howard Doane, two men who believed working for Jesus was a delight and a joy. Lowry would have preferred to have been known as a preacher but is now mostly remembered for his five hundred hymns. Doane, who was president of his father's company by the age of thirty-four, devoted almost as much time to his music as he did to his business. He was a genius at composition, and the team of W. H. Doane and the blind lyricist Fanny Crosby produced the most popular hymns of Mrs. Wilder's day. Indeed, an astonishing number of *Pure Gold*'s texts are still in hymnbooks even today.

"Rock of Ages," "Amazing Grace," "Revive Us Again," "Close to Thee," "A Mighty Fortress Is Our God," "Sweet Hour of Prayer," "Rescue the Perishing," "Jesus Loves Me (This I Know)," "How Sweet the Name of Jesus Sounds," "Savior, Like a Shepherd Lead Us," "Shall We Gather at the River?," "Jubilate Deo," and "Come, Thou Fount of Every Blessing" can all still be found in hymnals. And all these hymns had a profound influence in shaping the family values of their time. You can hear sermons and you can hear sermons, but evidence shows that most of us don't really remember sermons as much as we remember oft-repeated songs.

Melody, rhythm, and rhyme make words stick to the brain.

Songs of the Lord's Presence

The standards in *Pure Gold* assure that

> When gloomy clouds across the sky,
> Cast shadows o'er the land,
> Bright rays of light illume my path,
> For Jesus holds my hand.

The pioneers found they could endure almost any circumstance—even if they didn't know the reason behind it—if they felt God was present with them in "a mysterious way, His wonders to perform," as William Cowper said in his hymn. Maybe Jesus's hand was guiding, maybe only providing a feeling of presence, but the overpowering sense of divine company was the gist of many a hymn. The great unknowns of life can bring out a spirit of adventure in us, but all too often they only make us nervous, wary, and fearful. How about independent or self-reliant? Never entirely—we need the divine after all.

Christian, the lead character in John Bunyan's *Pilgrim's Progress,* has all his sins and the burden of them taken away at the cross, which comes early in his journey. But as a pilgrim he still has to make it to the Celestial City, so he is involved in encounters with Hypocrisy, Mistrust, Apollyon, Pagan, Talkative, and Vanity Fair. (What Bunyan would have thought of the secular magazine's appropriation of *Vanity Fair* one can only shudder to think!)

The Ingallses would have understood Christian's situation. And they would have known of *Pilgrim's Progress,* which in their time was the second most read book in America after the Bible. However, the question would have remained for them: Just how do I take Jesus's hand and go on with him? What does it mean to have God's presence *through* the journey?

A New Song

For the Ingallses, I believe what was of foremost importance was that they had a personal relationship with God through Jesus Christ. This was thought to be possible and was preached by the major revivalists and evangelicals of their era. This view was a great change from previous centuries when many of the great pulpiteers were more inclined to talk about God's attributes than about his personal and loving nature. From their viewpoint, God was angry at sinners and saints alike: at the sinner for being a sinner and at the saint for not being a "good enough" saint.

If the first awakening of American Protestant churches came in the 1750s under the influence of Jonathan Edwards, the second awakening came through the work of D. L. Moody. Moody became a traveling evangelist shortly before the start of the Civil War and continued his ministry until the end of the century.

Moody was a businessman turned lay preacher who once had headed the Chicago branch of the Young Men's Christian Association (YMCA). When he began his lay travels, guest speakers filled his home pulpit. One day a young fellow from England named Harry Moorhouse came asking to fill the pulpit. His only recommendation seems to have been a previous letter he had written to the evangelist on his own. Moody didn't quite know what to do, but while he was absent on yet another speaking engagement, his elders decided to let Moorhouse speak.

What Moorhouse preached was that contrary to the belief that God hated sinners, he actually loved them. Emma, Moody's wife, reported this to D. L., who then replied to her, "He is wrong." But the next Sunday, Moody heard Moorhouse preach for himself from the text "For God so loved the world . . ." (John 3:16). Moody later reported that the speaker "went from Genesis to Revelation giving proof that God loves the sinner, and before he got through, two or three of my sermons were spoiled."

Moody admitted, "I never knew up to that time that God loved us so much." The second great awakening was on its way. It was the awakening where we came to know that "Jesus holds my hand."

Songs of Promise

In the terrible year of 1876, Freddie Ingalls died. Pa and Ma's only son had never been strong, and he did not live out his first year. The loss of their son meant the Ingallses would never have that vital boy who would help his father feed the cattle and do the chores of the farm.

Then, in another terrible year, when family finances were still in bad shape from having to pay the doctor for trying to save Freddie, Mary became ill and eventually lost her sight. This was in 1879, and again the doctor's bills mounted. It would have been easy for the Ingallses to have thought themselves accursed by the time they came to the period depicted in Laura's *By the Shores of Silver Lake*. As it was, Mary never complained and the family continued to look forward with song. One such song of encouragement was "Mountain of the Lord" by Robert Lowry:

> Yes! a brighter morn is breaking,
> Better days are coming on;
> All the world will be awaking
> In the new and golden dawn.

> Refrain:
> And many nations shall come, and say,
> Come let us go up to the mountain of the Lord,
> Let us go up to the mountain of the Lord.

It can take a long time before the "brighter morn" breaks. Yet the Ingallses still could feel that they were part of a great dream to make America "a city upon a hill."

Although the hymn "Mountain of the Lord" is derived from the Old Testament (see Isaiah 2:2–3), the Ingallses would have regarded their efforts as part of bringing the kingdom of God to the prairies. The death of Freddie was tragic, but it was not God's judgment. Mary's blindness was a trial, but it was not the end. "All the world will be awaking in the new and golden dawn," but sometimes it takes the eyes of faith to see it.

The old hymns taught that being at peace with God does not mean one always has to understand the ways of God. Instead, hope is often focused on the belief that life will be better further on—sometimes all the way further on to heaven.

"The Happy Land" by Andrew Young, which is noted as "Ma's favorite" hymn by music historian Dr. Dale Cockrell, is found in the books *Little House on the Prairie, On the Banks of Plum Creek,* and *By the Shores of Silver Lake.* Laura and her sisters often sang,

> There is a happy land,
> Far, far away;
> Where saints in glory stand,
> Bright, bright as day. . . .
>
> Bright in that happy land
> Beams every eye;
> Kept by a Father's hand,
> Love cannot die.
> Oh, then, to glory run,
> Be a crown and kingdom won,
> And bright above the sun
> We reign for aye.

How different the pioneering perspective becomes from this point of view! Pioneers weren't exploiters of a virgin paradise, as some historians declared; they were visionaries bringing the kingdom of God to unsettled lands. The crown and the glory are abundant rewards for work well done against all odds.

The praise that was on the little family's lips was the praise of those who were counted worthy to suffer for such a cause. Mere personal gain didn't come into it. Pa wasn't going to become rich; he only wanted to prove he was a worthy pioneer. We know that Laura and Almanzo did not really prosper out west or even that much in the Ozarks, at least not through farming. But they expected the reward might come later on. One can work for an earthly paradise that isn't attained yet still believe that real happiness is found only in the hereafter. Laura could love the pioneer experience and still know this.

Spirituals for Work and Play

Oh, roll the ole chariot along,
Roll the ole chariot along,
Roll the ole chariot along,
If ye don't hang on behin'. . . .

Goin' to join with the hundred and forty-four thousand. . . .
If ye don't hang on behin'.

These words were sung as Pa and several others headed out for Volga, South Dakota, during the long winter of 1880–81. Regarded as a spiritual in most quarters, "Roll the Ole Chariot Along" probably found its way west as a work song to keep workers in rhythm as they swung picks and shovels or, in Pa's case, as men pumped a railroad handcart out to where others were working to clear the railroad line. The folks in De Smet needed the shipments of food and other supplies that would roll in from the East on trains.

The reference to joining the "hundred and forty-four thousand" echoes a reference in the Bible to the book of Revelation, where that number of God's followers come out of the "great tribulation" and are made "white in the blood of the Lamb" (see Revelation 7:4, 14). I hasten to add that these particular townsfolk were in no way thinking they were the fulfillment of this prophecy.

Although many groups did settle on the plains with the idea that they were in some way fulfilling God's coming millennium, there is no hint of this in Laura's writing. Rather, the important reason for men pumping a railcar to Volga in unison was so they could hurry to help get the snowbound train through.

Spirituals of the church served a similar purpose to our praise and worship songs today. There may not be much theology in repeating a chorus such as "Praise the Lord, O my soul, praise the Lord, O my soul. Bless his holy name." But an attitude of gratitude seems to arise from the mere act of repeating the words themselves. And it also occurs to me that the conflict we have in today's church between those who want to sing only praise songs and those who want to sing only the old hymns is not new. This sort of conflict must have gone on in previous times when some churches focused on singing only the words of the Psalms. Then came a time when reformer Martin Luther broke with that tradition by using all sorts of tunes for sacred purposes.

By today's standards we might find the tune to "A Mighty Fortress Is Our God" a bit stiff and even slow paced, but when Luther penned it, the song was considered revolutionary. Amazingly, this hymn remains in many a hymnal, while you won't find "Roll the Ole Chariot Along" except here and there in the spirituals section. It seems many praise songs seem to appeal only to the generation that first learned them.

For Laura, a song was a song and that was that; she loved to sing but was not a critic.

Songs for Head and Heart

Some have argued that a person needs praise songs for the heart and hymns for the head in order to be both a feeling and a thoughtful Christian. Surely head and heart Christianity must go together. The songbook *Pure Gold* doesn't contain "Roll the Ole Chariot Along," but it does contain the little tune "Jesus Loves Me," in which the familiar lyrics state,

> Jesus loves me! this I know,
> For the Bible tells me so.

This song seems to work for both head and heart and is no less popular now than in days gone by. In fact, most people now think of it as a hymn.

Spiritual meat for the soul in the Little House series comes from the previously mentioned "Rock of Ages," "Sweet Hour of Prayer," "Come, Thou Fount of Every Blessing," "Revive Us Again," and many other Ingalls family favorites. These hymns have substance in their content.

"Rock of Ages," by Augustus Toplady, pictures God not only as a cleft in the rock where one may hide from danger but also as the purifier of the soul. The water and blood that flowed from Jesus's side is for sin "the double cure," saving us from wrath and making us pure. That is, the believer is saved from sin eternally and also in his daily life. Not even one's own zeal or sorrow for sin can pay the price for wrongdoing. Rather, in the song's lyrics, "Thou must save, and Thou alone." God is an active God. Jesus was a sure and active refuge for a pioneering people.

Even in such mystical songs as "Be Still and Know" and "Sweet Hour of Prayer," God calls us "from a world of care" but also suggests we *do* have our part to play in our "world of care." We don't merely *wish* for help; we *call* upon the Father for what we need. Asking is a part of our "labor in the Lord" (1 Corinthians 15:58, NIV).

When Laura and her family prayed for help and protection, they knew they were not escapists but realists dealing with real dilemmas. It is obvious that composer William Walford, in "Sweet Hour of Prayer," was urging an active participation with those who await the Lord "with strong desires for thy return." To Walford, and to the pioneers who put their trust in God, to pray itself was a work of faith in which the believer demonstrated his or her obedience by seeking God's blessing (see Matthew 7:7–8, where the apostles are *told* to "ask," "seek," and "knock" and are promised "it shall be given you," "ye shall find," and "it shall be opened unto you").

This blended attitude of being still and knowing that God is God and that he is also the "rewarder of them that diligently seek him" (Hebrews 11:6) has been a challenge for Christians of every generation. It must be admitted that sometimes our forebears fell into the trap of saying "God helps those who help themselves"—popularized by Ben Franklin—when what they meant was "God helps those who especially need his help." The truly self-sufficient never think they have that need.

This was not a problem for the Ingalls family—they knew when their situation was dire and help was needed.

In *The Long Winter,* the bad weather of 1880–81 overwhelmed the whole town of De Smet. The trains had stopped running. The Ingallses were burning hay for warmth. The men were desperately hunting antelope and failing. Pa finally went to the Wilder boys, who were "batching it" in town, and bought some of Almanzo's seed wheat in order to feed the family. Real pioneers knew when they needed others.

Sometimes it is good to remember that the difficulties that face us are not really all that different from one generation to the next. Praise and "rest in God" songs can endure, but hymns often turn out to have more substance and structure if the writer is more content oriented in his or her lyrics.

Isaac Watts, God's Messenger

One such gifted writer who profoundly influenced Laura and her family was the composer and lyricist Isaac Watts. Though troubled throughout much of his life by mental illness, he wrote over 750 hymns, including this one that Ma Ingalls sings at the end of *The Long Winter:*

> When I can read my title clear
> to mansions in the skies,
> I'll bid farewell to every fear,
> and wipe my weeping eyes;
> and wipe my weeping eyes,
> and wipe my weeping eyes,
> I'll bid farewell to every fear,
> and wipe my weeping eyes. . . .

Let cares, like a wild deluge come,
and storms of sorrow fall!
May I but safely reach my home,
my God, my heaven, my all;
my God, my heaven, my all,
my God, my heaven, my all,
may I but safely reach my home,
my God, my heaven, my all.

The "title clear" of the song refers to the names of believers written in "the Lamb's book of life" (Revelation 21:27), and "mansions" refers to John 14:2. Another phrase in this song by Watts refers to "fiery darts," which is from Ephesians 6:16, and "Satan's rage" comes from 1 Peter 5:8 and refers to God's enemy, the devil, "seeking whom he may devour."

A great part of the pioneer's perspective on things was in keeping with the sober view that we live in a fallen world, which is seen in the song's phrase "a frowning world." Why is it a frowning world? Because of the fall of humankind into sin told of in the book of Genesis, which the pioneers would have been taught about in Sunday school, from the pulpit, and from their own personal experience. Laura's family, if anything, was very optimistic. You don't keep trying to settle again and again after setbacks unless you really believe, in the end, that there will be a great future provided by God somewhere. But their positive attitudes still would not have stopped them from singing about "a frowning world."

The truth is, the family's experience in Indian Territory had been a disaster—though perhaps Pa should have known better than to settle there. (He settled with an attitude of hope but with no title to the land.) Later, pioneering in Minnesota turned out to be a disaster too. The illness that took little Freddie's life and the plague of grasshoppers that took their crop—and ultimately the farm—could not have been anticipated, but it would have confirmed what they sang at night around the hearth about "a frowning world." Ultimately for the Ingallses, true hope in life and in death came from seeking "my home, my God, my heaven, my all," as Watts had penned.

No, the hymns that sang from Pa's fiddle were not merely distractions from challenging realities but the very essence of how to live an enduring life. This is a heritage of deepest profundity, and we would be wise to retain of it all that we can. It is the heritage of every American who believes, be they actual descendants of pioneers or not.

Isaac Watts and the Church Militant

Yet where today is the church militant, the church victorious? Certainly, the pioneers embraced that vision and sang of it. From the book *Little House in the Big Woods* comes a stanza from Isaac Watts's battle cry "Am I a Soldier of the Cross?"

> Am I a soldier of the cross,
> A follower of the Lamb,
> And shall I fear to own His cause,
> Or blush to speak His Name?

How strange these words must sound to those whose hymnals no longer include hymns like "Onward, Christian Soldiers." Although spiritual warfare isn't won by literal swords (see Ephesians 6:17), it won't be won by denying there is a battle either. Also, these words are a reminder that Christianity isn't about swimming with the tide but swimming against it. The reference to blushing at the name of Christ reminds us of the timidity from which we must be delivered if we are to bear his name. Spiritual courage is a necessary virtue for victory.

Of course, we might well wish it otherwise, and Watts painted an almost humorous picture of a sheltered soldier in the stanza quoted in *Little House in the Big Woods:*

Shall I be carried to the skies,
On flowery beds of ease,
While others fought to win the prize,
And sailed through bloody seas?

One can hardly imagine Laura's pastor, the Reverend Edward Brown, being someone taking the easy way! Reverend Brown was paid next to nothing by his poor congregation, and if he hadn't had a little steel in his backbone, he wouldn't have dragged his family out west. It is significant that he made his own homestead claim. Certainly, there was no flowery bed of ease for him, and he could well identify with what his own parishioners faced.

The now-popular idea that if I follow God he will give me my wants, dreams, and wishes must have developed well after the pioneer period ended. It is revealing that the anniversary issue of the *De Smet News* in 1930, fifty years after the founding of the town, was full of advertising from a number of grocery stores, hardware stores, and clothing shops—all in a still relatively modest-sized municipality. It turns out that fifty years later there was more to want than in pioneer days, and "flowery beds of ease" seemed just around the corner. The paper boasted of De Smet's prosperity and prominence, but one has to wonder what returning old-timers must have felt.

In Watts's hymn there is another question:

Are there no foes for me to face?
Must I not stem the flood?
Is this vile world a friend to grace,
To help me on to God?

One can suspect an old settler might have felt that the younger generation had gone soft, with modern hard-won luxuries now being seen as common goods. Mrs. Wilder, for one, had such thoughts. In a *Missouri Ruralist* column from the 1920s, she wrote, "When tests of character come in later years, strength to the good will not come from the modern improvements [such as "motor cars or radio outfits"] . . . but from the quiet moments and the 'still small voices' of the old home." Among these voices was the echo of oft-sung hymns that warned that life was more than having ordinary bread and worldly goods.

Isaac Watts and Eternity

The pioneers were looking for more than material success; they desired heavenly success as well. Their faith and conscience told them that the battle was not to the strong but to the enduring. Watts's hymn continues,

Sure I must fight, if I would reign:
Increase my courage, Lord;
I'll bear the toil, endure the pain,
Supported by Thy word.

And this the Ingallses did although they didn't always see the fruits of their efforts, any more than the prophets of the Old Testament did. The epistle to the Hebrews reminds us, "These all died in faith [Abel, Enoch, Noah, Abraham, Isaac, Jacob, and Sarah], not having received the promises, but having seen them afar off, and were persuaded of them, and embraced them, and confessed that they were strangers and pilgrims on the earth" (11:13).

Perhaps the children of pioneers did, in fact, receive more of a temporal reward than the first pioneers. Certainly, children are always building on the opportunities provided by their parents. Watts made it clear that there remained a heavenly reward for those first settlers who had to be so heavenly minded.

> Thy saints in all this glorious war
> Shall conquer, though they die;
> They see the triumph from afar,
> By faith they bring it nigh.

There remains, then, a "rest to the people of God" (Hebrews 4:9). They have ceased from their labors, and their works *do* follow them.

> When that illustrious day shall rise,
> And all Thy armies shine
> In robes of victory through the skies,
> The glory shall be Thine.

Truly, Watts was a profound inspiration to the Ingalls family but also to pioneers all over the West. His hymns were found in hundreds of denominational and nondenominational hymnals of the day. But his grand influence may have been second on the list of family favorites after another songwriter: Fanny Crosby.

Fanny Crosby, Hymn Writer to the Country

I believe Fanny Crosby was the most influential of any hymn writer to the pioneers. Although Isaac Watts wrote hundreds of hymns, despite terrifying bouts of mental illness, Crosby wrote thousands of hymns, some nine thousand in all, in spite of her blindness. No less than thirty of her hymns are in *Pure Gold*. The publishers of *Pure Gold* took a shortcut with the hymn that advises "Cling Closer to Jesus" by simply noting "words by Fannie," as though everyone ought to know who Fanny is.

Crosby wrote numerous songs for Sunday school, and one of the songs the Ingallses no doubt sang—as they often kept Sunday school at home during times when they weren't near a church—was "Our Sabbath Home," which is so characteristic of Fanny's lyrics. (The tune was by her pastor, Robert Lowry.)

> Joyful once again we sing,
> In our Sabbath Home;
> Praise to God our Saviour King,
> In our Sabbath Home.
> While before His throne we bend,
> While our prayers to Him ascend,
> Pleasant is the time we spend,
> In our Sabbath Home. . . .

If we truly seek His face,
He will fill this sacred place
With the light of heavenly grace,
In our Sabbath Home.

There are at least two stories in the Little House series that tell of how boring Sunday seemed to be to children. In *Little House in the Big Woods*, Laura gets rebellious about not being able to run around and play on Sunday. Pa tells her a story of just how strict Sunday used to be when his own father was a boy. Back then, the Sabbath began on Saturday evening after the sun went down, and no food could be prepared at all on the Sabbath. Almanzo had also learned from his experiences that Sunday could be a dreadful day. The Wilders mostly spent the day reading the Bible or sitting until they fell asleep.

One has to wonder if Crosby wrote this chorus as part of an effort to make the solemn day more cheerful. Perhaps words like "Pleasant is the time we spend" were meant to remind fidgety children that active worship could bring good feelings as well as somber ones. "The light of heavenly grace" could fill the home with a kind of sanctity. I believe many people reading Laura's books do realize there was an essence of goodness that surrounded the Ingalls family as they worshipped God at home as well as at church.

Musicologist Dale Cockrell wrote of Laura's prairie stories, "Given the books' subject matter and their extraordinary popularity, one might say without hyperbole that there may be no narratives more responsible for establishing and maintaining the popular mythology of the 'Great American Family' than the Little House novels." To Dr. Cockrell, who has made three CDs of the music the Ingalls family sang, there are "moral and character lessons aplenty," as demonstrated by their times around Pa's fiddle and in their choice of songs. (Dr. Cockrell's work can be found at www.laura-ingalls-wilder.com/index.htm.)

Indeed, in *Little Town on the Prairie* we find the little family more involved in church and worship than ever as they go to service and Sunday school in the morning and then to afternoon church to finish the day. Hymn 18 in *Pure Gold* was a favorite of Laura's. The title is "The Good Old Way," with lyrics by Fanny Crosby and music by W. H. Doane:

We are going forth with our staff in hand,
Thro' a desert wild in a stranger land;
But our faith is bright and our hope is strong,
And the Good Old Way is our pilgrim song.

The scriptural reference is to John 14:6, where Jesus says to his disciples that he is "the way, the truth, and the life: no man cometh unto the Father, but by me." This path is the "Good Old Way" because it was handed down to the Ingallses by their own pioneer ancestors. People going west found it easy to believe they were really on the pathway to a righteous kingdom because they were bringing culture and Christianity to "a desert wild in a stranger land," just a little farther on than their parents had traveled. Crosby's song goes on to say, "There are foes without, there are foes within." No matter; the good old way of holy example taught what they needed to know of morals and of God.

Laura once wrote, "I realize that all my life the teachings of those early [pioneer] days have influenced me, and . . . [have] been something I have tried to follow, with failures here and there, with rebellion at times; but always coming back to it as the compass needle to the star."

Merry, Merry Christmas

The reason there are so many Christmas stories in the Little House series is because the theme of Christmas charity was a unifying tradition in the Ingalls family. A centerpiece of each of the eight books in the series is some special celebration of Christmas, which depicts the virtues of giving and sacrifice as being of highest value. And, as always, there was song.

One particularly memorable Christmas is recorded in *By the Shores of Silver Lake.* Rob and Ella Boast arrive just at Christmastime to beat the rush of settlers who will soon be coming in their wake. Mr. and Mrs. Boast are friends of the Ingalls family and were later described as the closest friends Pa and Ma ever had. Interestingly, not one of the songs mentioned in this episode, except "Jingle Bells," is one we would likely sing today. The one song sung by the Ingallses and the Boasts that is recorded went,

> Merry, merry Christmas everywhere!
> Cheerily it ringeth through the air;
> Christmas bells, Christmas trees,
> Christmas odors on the breeze. . . .
>
> Why should we so joyfully
> Sing with grateful mirth?
> See! the Sun of Righteousness
> Beams upon the earth!

A number of Sunday school books of the period include this song, and it probably was written by a woman in New England who was familiar with the bells and trees of her area. A true Christmas tree was impossible to find on the prairie, and in 1879 there was no town yet for the Boasts and the Ingallses, let alone a church or bells or trees, except for the lone cottonwood by Lake Henry. There weren't enough gifts for everyone either. The Boasts had not come prepared for Christmas, though Mr. Boast was able to provide the girls with some Christmas candy. Christ was definitely in Christmas back then.

The season was joyful because it celebrated the "Sun of Righteousness," who came as a child to be born so that his teachings and influence would shed "beams upon the earth." Even though they had so little, as Laura emphasized in all her Christmas stories, they really had much in God's gift of his Son. People who don't expect much at Christmas may be inclined to be less needy by way of material wants.

Interestingly, in the Little House series there is no reference to one of Christmas's most popular hymns, Watts's "Joy to the World," though it was well known at the time. Of course, strictly speaking, Watts's hymn isn't a Christmas song but a hymn about Christ's reign on earth at his second coming. Nevertheless, it was almost immediately adopted as a Christmas song and did appear in the 1878 *Hymnal of the Methodist Episcopal Church,* which is what the Ingalls family probably used. The song was also undoubtedly in the Congregational hymnal of Laura's day. As to how this second-coming song came to be attached to Christmas, no one seems to know.

In any case, two additional songs the Ingallses associated with Christmas adorn *By the Shores of Silver Lake:* "Mountain of the Lord" and "Gentle Words and Loving Smiles." "Mountain of the Lord" I referred to earlier, and it appears in the *Pure Gold* hymnal. It turns out to be another second-coming song used at Christmas to celebrate the first Advent. The Scripture passage it is based on is Isaiah 2:2–3:

And it shall come to pass in the last days, that the mountain of the LORD's house shall be established in the top of the mountains, and shall be exalted above the hills; and all nations shall flow unto it. . . .

And he will teach us of his ways, and we will walk in his paths: for out of Zion shall go forth the law, and the word of the LORD from Jerusalem.

Here I suspect the phrase "and he will teach us of his ways" is crucial to the meaning of the hymn in that now we have in Jesus Christ the One who will "make straight in the desert a highway for our God" (Isaiah 40:3) in the "last days," as referred to in the text from Isaiah 2.

To the pioneers, their era must have seemed like some kind of fulfillment of prophecy. The Word of the Lord was spreading as they settled a wilderness. A nation that lived according to God's laws, as they felt America did, was leading the world into an era in which Christ's reign would finally be made manifest.

The plowman supplants the soldier because Christ has brought peace on earth and goodwill to men. Therefore, the Ingallses must have felt at times that they had a high and holy duty in accomplishing God's plan for the earth.

Lastly, the words from "Gentle Words and Loving Smiles" by Robert Lowry close out the *Silver Lake* Christmas:

It is not much the world can give
With all its subtle art;
And gold and gems are not the things
To satisfy the heart;

But Oh, if those who cluster round
The altar and the hearth,
Have gentle words and loving smiles,
How beautiful the earth!

Pa's fiddle had led them from a theme of fulfilled prophecy to a theme of sacred home life. Happy is the home when God is there. God's grand vision includes the home: the peace and security of it, the perspectives of it when we cease striving for earthly gold, the happiness of it when we perceive its pleasures as a foretaste of heaven.

It was, indeed, fortunate that Pa's hopes ultimately centered on a heavenly reward. His earthly efforts, in the end, probably disappointed him. He and Ma and Mary spent their last years in the town of De Smet after Pa moved the family from the farm in 1888, only two years after he "proved up"—served his five years—on his homestead claim in 1886. The homestead itself was apparently sold in 1892. The family then became firmly attached to the little town they'd helped establish but hadn't planned to live in. No matter how he may have felt about leaving the claim, Pa lived on as one of De Smet's most distinguished citizens.

Efforts to trace what Pa did for a living in town have proved difficult. Since he had skills as a carpenter, he could have worked in that profession. And there is even a possibility that he may have had a store, for Ma Ingalls is reported to have done supplemental sewing, using material from supplies Pa had on hand when he passed away.

Pa died in 1902 at the age of sixty-six. Part of his obituary reads,

As a citizen he was held in high esteem, being honest and
upright in his dealings and associations with his fellows. As

a friend and neighbor he was always kind and courteous and
as a husband and father he was faithful and loving. And what
better can be said of any man? Some few accomplish great
things in life's short span; they control the destinies of nations,
or hold in their hand, as it were, the wealth of the world; but the
great many tread the common walks of life and to them falls the
work of making the world better. He who does this work well is
the truly great man. Such was he who has lately been called to
the Great Beyond. Charles P. Ingalls did his life's work well and
the world is better for his having lived in it.

Things were never the same for the Ingalls family. Of course, by
then Laura had married Almanzo, given birth to Rose, and moved
away. She returned from Mansfield to be with her father at his death,
and she inherited his fiddle as her only memento of him other than
what she carried in her heart.

Hopefully this was comfort enough as she looked back over her life
as an Ingalls. Pa's earthly prosperity had been meager, at best, his heavenly prosperity more real and considerable. Fittingly, Pa's favorite hymn
was sung at his funeral. It was "In the Sweet By and By."

There's a land that is fairer than day,
And by faith we can see it afar;
For the Father waits over the way
To prepare us a dwelling place there.

In the sweet by and by
We shall meet on that beautiful shore;

In the sweet by and by
We shall meet on that beautiful shore.

The struggle was over, the pioneer was at rest, the heritage was passed on—a common heritage for us all.

The Church Potluck

Thinking of pies and poems, I am more content with pie making for surely it is better to make a good pie than a poor poem.

—LAURA INGALLS WILDER

Any small church worth its salt during the 1950s through the early 1970s when I was growing up offered potluck dinners as a way to increase fellowship and share a time reflective of the Lord's heavenly banquet table. True, the fare was humble, but it was also plenteous, and all of it—at least in my own experience—was full of what made food so tasty back then: salt, fat, and sugar! Everyone had a fried chicken recipe, and ham was the other choice of meat. Casseroles were swimming in cream of mushroom soup. There were homemade dinner rolls, pies, and cupcakes. Life was good.

In the '70s, I gradually noticed a cultural shift as I left my country home and moved to Kansas City and much larger churches. The church potluck was still popular, and eating was still a good excuse for fellowship. You could meet and be friendly and not have to put on a pious face. But somehow Kentucky Fried Chicken had crept into the menu for those folk who, busy working two or three jobs, didn't have time to resort to their inherited fried chicken recipes. For a time Colonel Sanders fought it out with the traditional homemade fried chicken—and then things changed completely, as more and more churches resorted to catering their "potlucks." Women simply couldn't handle the baby, their jobs, and their husbands, and still find time to cook. As for men, at that time, only a few admitted to cooking. Grilling, yes; cooking, no.

So let us return to an even earlier time when we were pioneers on the prairie, when women weren't supposed to work outside the home—although they did anyway—and when every one of them was a terrific cook (either that or their men were in a really bad way, because I never heard any farmer from where I grew up admit to being able to cook).

All of the following recipes are authentic and come from people who knew Laura and her parents during their De Smet church days. Indeed, these recipes were gathered by the early Congregational church that both Mary and Ma attended for many years after Laura and Almanzo had decided to try their fortunes in Missouri.

The *Cream City Cook Book* was published in 1914, and you will find here many recipes by familiar names from the Little House books: Mrs. Rob Boast, Ma's dear friend; Mrs. F. C. Bradley, the druggist's singing wife; Mrs. C. S. G. Fuller, whose husband owned a hardware store; Mrs. D. H. Loftus, whose husband tried to charge a high price for wheat in *The Long Winter;* and Ma Ingalls herself, with a recipe for a kind of relish/slaw.

You Are a Pioneer Now

I say the recipes are "authentic." By this I mean that the measuring of ingredients and the instructions for blending have been adapted by my sister, Jane, great cook that she is, to give a result similar to what the pioneers themselves expected. So if you are looking for fluffy frostings for these cake recipes, for example, expunge the thought. The frostings here turn out to be rather thin affairs compared to what we are used to today. Fix, eat, and be satisfied. You are a pioneer now.

And please forgive Jane and me for the heating instructions: ovens do vary, and the original instructions were cruelly imprecise. We have tried to make the temperature correct for you. You won't be too far off, and the pioneers weren't expecting perfection anyway. They had to eat their failures as well as their successes. Back then, you simply didn't throw food away.

Mrs. Rob Boast

Mrs. Rob Boast was Ma's first and best friend in the new settlement of De Smet. The Boasts arrived for the winter of 1879 to get a jump on others soon to make a home on the prairie. They always lived on their claim after that winter and, thus, went through the hard winter of 1880–81 out on their farm. We don't know, but perhaps their house was made of sod. Such houses were common and much warmer than the typical thin claim shanty that would have been dreadful to live in during any season.

🌿 GINGER CAKE

3 cups flour
1 teaspoon baking soda
1 teaspoon ginger

1 teaspoon cinnamon

1 teaspoon cloves

1 cup sugar

2/3 cup butter or shortening

1 cup brown sugar dissolved in 1/2 cup hot water

2 eggs

1 cup milk

Sift flour, soda, ginger, cinnamon, and cloves. Set aside.

Cream sugar and shortening. Add brown sugar mixture, eggs, and milk and mix. Stir in dry ingredients.

Pour into a greased and floured 9 x 13-inch baking pan. Bake at 350 degrees for 35 to 40 minutes.

Nut Cake

2 1/2 cups flour

1 tablespoon baking powder

1/2 cup butter

1 1/2 cups sugar

3 eggs

1/2 cup milk

1 cup chopped nuts

Sift 1/2 cup of flour with baking powder and set aside.

Cream butter and sugar until very light. Add eggs and beat. Add remaining flour and milk and beat. Stir in nuts.

Grease and flour a 9 x 13-inch baking pan. Just before pouring batter into pan, stir in sifted 1/2 cup flour and baking powder. Bake at 350 degrees for 25 to 30 minutes.

🌿 DOUGHNUTS

1 cup sour milk
2 eggs
1 1/2 cups sugar
2 tablespoons melted shortening
1 teaspoon baking soda
Pinch of salt
1/8 teaspoon nutmeg
5 1/2 cups flour

To make sour milk, place 1 tablespoon lemon juice or vinegar in a measuring cup and add milk to make 1 cup. Set aside a few minutes to sour.

Beat eggs. Add sugar, sour milk, melted shortening, soda, salt, and nutmeg and stir. Stir in flour to form a stiff, sticky dough. Toss lightly on a floured surface and roll out 1/2-inch thick. Cut with doughnut cutter.

Heat fat or vegetable oil 3 to 4 inches deep in a heavy kettle (or deep-fat fryer) to 375 degrees. Fry doughnuts a few minutes on each side to a light golden brown.

[Or give yourself a rest and remember that Krispy Kreme doughnuts are perfectly welcome at church these days.]

Mrs. C. L. Dawley

Attending the De Smet Congregational church was Mrs. C. L. Dawley, who, prior to getting married, was Florence Garland, Laura's first teacher in the town. Her brother, Cap Garland, was an early romantic interest of Laura's. Almanzo and Cap went out in search of wheat during the hard winter.

❧ BLACK CHOCOLATE CAKE

1/2 cup cocoa

3/4 cup and 2 tablespoons hot water

1 cup sour milk

1/2 cup butter

2 cups light brown sugar

2 eggs

2 cups flour

1 teaspoon baking soda

1 teaspoon baking powder

Dissolve cocoa in hot water. Set aside to cool.

To make sour milk, place 1 tablespoon lemon juice or vinegar in a measuring cup and add milk to make 1 cup. Set aside a few minutes to sour.

Cream butter, sugar, and eggs. Beat in dissolved cocoa.

Sift together flour, soda, and baking powder. Add to batter alternately with sour milk.

Pour into a greased and floured 9 x 13-inch baking pan.

Bake at 350 degrees for 30 to 35 minutes until toothpick
inserted in center comes out clean and cake begins to pull
away from edges of pan.

🌿 APPLE CHARLOTTE

Butter a deep baking dish. Cover bottom with a layer of
sliced, peeled apples. Add a layer of buttered stale bread
crumbs, then a layer of apples sprinkled with sugar and a little
cinnamon. Continue layering bread crumbs, apples, and sugar
and cinnamon until dish is full, using apples for the top layer.
Moisten with hot water and bake, covered, until apples are
done (about 40 minutes at 350 degrees for a 9-inch loaf pan).
Uncover and bake until browned, 10 minutes. Serve warm
with sugar and cream.

🌿 CRANBERRY PIE

11/4 cups split cranberries
Water
11/4 cups sugar
2 tablespoons flour
2-crust 9-inch pie shell

Measure cranberries and add water to measuring cup to
cover cranberries. Combine sugar and flour in a mixing
bowl and add cranberries. Pour into pie shell. Cover

with top crust. Cut steam vents. Bake at 425 degrees
for 30 to 40 minutes or until juice bubbles and crust is
browned.

We now begin to ease our way into some bread recipes. Mrs.
Dawley's Graham Gems aren't difficult, really, but wait till you see
some of the others! When mass baking came along and women could
go to the grocery and buy bread for a week, they felt liberated indeed!
Otherwise bread making was often a daily chore and kneading dough
was especially hard on hands and wrists.

🌿 GRAHAM GEMS

1 cup sour milk
1/2 cup sour cream
1/2 cup molasses
1 teaspoon soda
1 teaspoon salt
11/2 cups whole wheat flour
3/4 cup white flour

To make sour milk, place 1 tablespoon lemon juice or vinegar
in a measuring cup and add milk to make 1 cup. Set aside a
few minutes to sour.

Mix sour milk, sour cream, and molasses in a small bowl.
Combine soda, salt, whole wheat flour, and white flour in a
mixing bowl. Add combined liquids all at once to dry
ingredients. Mix only until all ingredients are moistened.

Fill greased muffin cups two-thirds full. Bake at 400 degrees for 20 to 25 minutes. Cool briefly in cups and then turn out on rack or towel.

[Note: There are no eggs or oil in this recipe.]

Mrs. F. C. Bradley

Mrs. F. C. Bradley, singer and organ player for De Smet's literaries, moved Ma and Laura to tears with her singing. May this graham loaf not move you to tears as you steam your way to bread.

❧ STEAM GRAHAM LOAF

2 cups sour milk

1 cup molasses

1/2 cup sugar

1 teaspoon salt

1/2 teaspoon baking powder

1 teaspoon baking soda dissolved in 1 tablespoon
    boiling water

1/2 cup white flour

3 cups whole wheat flour

To make sour milk, place 2 tablespoons lemon juice in a quart measuring cup and add milk to make 2 cups. Set aside a few minutes to sour.

To make batter, mix ingredients in the order listed. Pour into four well-greased No. 2 cans. (Cans containing

20 ounces of fruit are usually No. 2 cans.) Fill cans 2/3 full or slightly less. Cover cans with double thickness of waxed paper and fasten in place with rubber bands. The paper prevents steam that collects on the kettle's cover from falling onto the bread.

Place cans on a trivet in a deep kettle with a tight-fitting lid. (If you use a steamer, follow the manufacturer's directions.)

Pour boiling water to halfway up the sides of the cans. Steam for 2 1/2 hours.

Remove cans from kettle and remove paper from tops. Place cans in a very hot oven (450 degrees) for 5 minutes. Cut out end of can with can opener and push out loaf. Slice with a heavy thread drawn around the loaf, crossing ends. Serve hot.

To reheat cooled or frozen bread, place in a colander and cover with a clean dish towel. Steam 15 minutes over boiling water until hot.

[Note: To heat frozen loaf in a microwave, unwrap bread and place on a plate. Cover with waxed paper. Microwave on 50 percent power for 6 to 8 minutes. Let stand 5 minutes before slicing.]

Mrs. C. S. G. Fuller

Mrs. C. S. G. Fuller's husband was the clog-dancing minstrel in *Little Town on the Prairie,* and Mrs. Fuller was well known to the Ingalls family, being active in church and community affairs. When De Smet began having Old Settlers Day Celebrations, the Fullers were always remembered as prominent in town history.

🌿 ROLLS

4 cups milk

1/2 cup shortening

1/2 cup sugar

1 tablespoon salt

2 packages dry yeast

1 cup warm water

9 1/2 to 10 1/2 cups bread flour

1/2 cup melted butter or margarine

Scald milk and pour over shortening, sugar, and salt in a very large mixing bowl. Cool to room temperature. Dissolve yeast in water. (The water needs to be lukewarm—just warm enough to dissolve the yeast.) Add yeast to cooled milk mixture. Add 6 1/2 cups flour to make a stiff batter. Cover and let rise until doubled and bubbly, about 2 hours.

Stir down mixture and add enough flour to make a soft dough, 3 to 4 cups. Turn out on floured surface and knead 15 minutes. Clean bowl and grease lightly. Return dough to bowl, turning to grease top. Let rise until doubled, about 1 1/2 hours.

Divide dough in half and roll to 1/2-inch thickness. Cut with a 3-inch round biscuit cutter. Brush with melted butter, fold over, and press to seal edges. Place on greased baking sheets.

Cover and let rise until doubled, about 30 minutes. Bake at 375 degrees for 12 to 15 minutes. Remove from baking sheet and brush tops with melted butter.

[Note: Because you set a sponge in this recipe by first making a pre-fermented smaller part of the larger dough, it is

important not to start with your liquids too warm or your first
rising will be too fast. Also, do not use quick-rise yeast. The
high gluten in bread flour will also help your bread be light
through all the risings. Mrs. Fuller said this recipe would make
4 dozen rolls. When we tested the recipe, it made 4 dozen rolls
and a 9 x 13-inch pan of cinnamon rolls, our recipe!]

❧ White Cake

2 1/2 cups flour
2 teaspoons baking powder
1/2 cup butter
1 1/2 cups sugar
1 cup milk or water
5 egg whites
1 1/2 cups chopped nuts (optional)

Sift flour and baking powder and set aside.

Cream butter and gradually add sugar. Add flour
mixture alternately with milk. Beat entire mixture for 5
minutes. Beat egg whites until stiff and fold into batter. Pour
into two greased and floured 8-inch round cake pans or one
9 x 13-inch baking pan.

Bake at 350 degrees for 25 to 30 minutes. Cool for 10
minutes. Turn out on cooling racks.

(To make a nut cake, add chopped nuts before folding in
egg whites.)

🌿 CREAM PIE

1¹/2 cups half-and-half

2 egg yolks (save whites for meringue)

1/2 cup sugar

2 teaspoons cornstarch

1 teaspoon vanilla

1 baked 8-inch pie shell

2 tablespoons sugar

Heat half-and-half in top of double boiler. Combine egg yolks, 1/2 cup sugar, and cornstarch. Add to half-and-half. Cook, stirring constantly, until thick and smooth. Remove from heat. Add vanilla.

Stir until smooth and blended. Pour hot filling into pie shell.

For meringue, beat egg whites until stiff, gradually adding 2 tablespoons sugar. Heap on top of pie. Place in 350 degree oven to brown for 10 to 15 minutes.

🌿 CUCUMBER PICKLES

4 cups pickling salt

2 gallons water

2 gallons small whole cucumbers

1/2 cup white mustard seed

2 tablespoons whole allspice

2 tablespoons peppercorns

2 tablespoons whole cloves

3/4 cup broken cinnamon sticks

6 cups vinegar

3 red peppers, cut in chunks

A few pieces of fresh horseradish

2 cups brown sugar

1 cup molasses

Dissolve pickling salt in water. Add cucumbers and soak for three days in a stone crock or glass, pottery, or unchipped enamel-lined pan. Place a plate almost as large as the crock over the cucumbers and lay something heavy on top to keep cucumbers under the brine.

On the fourth day, rinse pickles well and wipe dry.

Tie mustard seed, allspice, peppercorns, cloves, and cinnamon sticks in a cloth bag. Boil spices in 1 cup vinegar, along with red pepper and horseradish.

Add spiced vinegar to remaining vinegar and brown sugar and bring to a boil. Pour over cucumbers, adding more vinegar if needed to cover. Weigh down cucumbers with a plate as before.

On each of days four through ten, drain off vinegar and scald. Pour again over cucumbers. Weigh down.

On the eleventh day, drain off vinegar and add molasses before scalding. Pack cucumbers in hot, sterilized glass jars. Pour hot syrup over cucumbers to cover. Seal. Process jars in boiling water bath (212 degrees) for 5 minutes.

[This is almost like one of those long-range class projects you used to have at school, but this is the sort of activity that pioneer women filled their days with, and all for pickles!]

Ma Ingalls

Here is another recipe for pickles that tells you there have been some changes in the American language as time has gone by. Today, Ma Ingalls's recipe would be regarded as more of a slaw, a frequent potluck offering. Caroline Lake Quiner Ingalls would most likely have grown her own cabbage and tomatoes. Served in a variety of ways, they would have been stalwarts at the Ingallses' table.

MIXED PICKLES

1 gallon chopped cabbage
1 gallon green tomatoes
1 quart onions
3 green peppers
1/2 cup pickling salt
4 tablespoons ground mustard seed
2 tablespoons ginger
1 tablespoon cloves
1 tablespoon cinnamon
1 tablespoon allspice
6 cups sugar

1 ounce celery seed

6 cups vinegar

Chop cabbage, tomatoes, onions, and peppers. Sprinkle with salt and let stand an hour or two. Press out water.

Mix in mustard seed, ginger, cloves, cinnamon, allspice, sugar, celery seed, and 6 cups vinegar or enough to cover vegetables. Boil slowly for 20 minutes.

Pour into hot, sterilized glass jars. Seal. Process jars in boiling water bath (212 degrees) for 5 minutes.

By now the inquiring mind might say, "Perhaps catering a meal makes a whole lot more sense than going to the trouble that these people did?" Certainly, the thought has occurred to me. But then we must remember that the whole of what church was about included an element of entertainment and pleasure that we simply don't quite understand in our day of many other kinds of diversions. I started to lose an interest in Sunday evening church services when Walt Disney began to run his *Wonderful World of Color* at the same time as youth group. Oh, the temptations of Disney and color!

So Many Desserts,
So Little Time

How to explain all the desserts among the recipes of the Congregational church's cookbook? I can only guess. For one thing, many of De Smet's settlers were originally from New England, and the New England tradition contains a regular staple of pies to be served with breakfast. (Why we don't do this anymore, I don't know.) Dessert may just have been a substantial part of what these women had learned to cook. It is also true that dietary information was primitive; there was a danger from malnutrition, but who would have guessed it? The men and women worked so hard physically that they just didn't gain the weight we would have on this dessert-rich diet.

Finally, I must admit that the women providing these recipes— women who would have been known to the young Laura—didn't provide recipes for very many of their meat dishes. I don't know why. Maybe in those days you just boiled or fried the meat with enough salt and lard, and that was the recipe. Whatever the reason, the *Cream City Cook Book* has pages and pages of sweet things to eat and only a page and a half for meat dishes, which I could sum up by saying just be sure to cook until well done; medium well does not seem to have been a practice of those days.

Mrs. F. L. Harthorn

To start off our dessert theme, we now come to Mrs. F. L. Harthorn's contributions. The Harthorns were a prominent town family, and Harthorn's dry-goods store was one of the earliest businesses in De Smet. The Harthorns were also among the band of eighty families who endured the hard winter together. The Harthorn store was less than half a block from the house Pa Ingalls built on Second Street.

POPCORN BALLS

3 gallons popped corn
2 cups sugar

1 cup water

1/2 teaspoon cream of tartar

Sort out any unpopped kernels and place popped corn in a very large container. Boil sugar, water, and cream of tartar to hard ball stage (250 to 266 degrees on a candy thermometer).

Pour syrup over popped corn, stirring quickly to coat. Make into balls as fast as possible, keeping hands moist by dipping them often in cold water.

[Note: While the syrup did not coat this amount of popcorn well, it did coat it enough to be able to form the mixture into balls. You might want to add 1 teaspoon vanilla to the syrup for flavoring.]

French Cream Cake

3 eggs, separated

1 cup sugar

11/2 cups flour

1 teaspoon baking powder

4 tablespoons water

1 teaspoon vanilla

Beat egg yolks and sugar. Add flour, baking powder, water, and vanilla. Beat egg whites until stiff and fold into batter. Bake in a greased and floured loaf pan at 350 degrees for 40 to 45 minutes.

[Note: The original instructions said to bake in a loaf pan or three layer pans. The recipe did not make enough batter to fill even two layer pans. The ingredients do not include shortening, so the cake was very dry and tough. Good luck! Who said every church lady was a good cook?]

Mrs. D. H. Loftus

Mr. D. H. Loftus was another very early settler of the town and tried to make a profit off the bravery of Almanzo and Cap Garland's trip to find wheat for the starving citizens during the hard winter. Loftus backed off his high-priced demands to stay in good standing with his customers. As for Mrs. Loftus, she kept to her cooking.

WHITE LAYER CAKE

11/2 cups flour
1 teaspoon baking soda
1 teaspoon cream of tartar
1/2 cup butter
1 cup sugar
1/2 cup milk
4 egg whites, beaten very stiff

Sift flour, soda, and cream of tartar. Set aside.

Cream butter and sugar. Add milk and beat. Add egg whites and sifted flour mixture and beat for 3 minutes.

Pour batter into a greased and floured 9 x 13-inch pan or two 8-inch round cake pans. Bake at 350 degrees for 15 to 20 minutes.

[Note: This cake was put together following the directions Mrs. Loftus provided in the recipe. All the air beaten into the egg whites was, of course, beaten out in the 3 minutes at the end. It made a quite thin 9 x 13-inch cake. One wonders if the egg whites should have been folded in *after* the flour was beaten into the batter. Try that for better results.]

❧ SEA FOAM CANDY

2 cups brown sugar
1/2 cup water
1 egg white
1 teaspoon vanilla
1/2 cup chopped nuts

Boil brown sugar and water to soft ball stage (235 to 240 degrees on a candy thermometer).

Stiffly beat egg white. Pour boiling syrup over egg white in a steady stream, continuing to beat constantly. When it gets a little stiff, add vanilla and chopped nuts.

When the mixture will stand alone, drop by rounded spoonfuls on waxed paper or a buttered pan. Store tightly covered.

🌿 PEACH AND ORANGE CONSERVE

12 peaches

6 oranges

7 cups sugar

2 cups water

2 cups blanched almonds, chopped

Peel and cut up peaches. Grate rind from oranges, using none of the white. Cut pulp into slices.

Cook peaches, oranges, grated rind, sugar, and water until thick and clear. Add almonds 15 minutes before removing from heat. Pour into hot jars; seal. Makes ten small jars.

🌿 GOOSEBERRY CONSERVE

6 quarts gooseberries

6 oranges

4 cups raisins

24 cups sugar

Grind gooseberries and oranges (rind and all). Add raisins and sugar. Stir to combine. Bring mixture to a boil. Cook over low heat, stirring frequently, until thick. Pour into hot jars; seal.

[If you've ever eaten a single wild gooseberry, you'll know

why the 24 cups of sugar are necessary. Keep this entirely out
of the reach of diabetics!]

🌿 Doughnuts

....

1 teaspoon baking soda
1 teaspoon cinnamon
1/8 teaspoon nutmeg
3 1/2 cups flour
2/3 cup sugar
4 tablespoons melted butter
2 eggs
1 cup buttermilk

Sift soda, cinnamon, nutmeg, and flour together. Set aside.

Beat sugar, melted butter, and eggs. Add buttermilk. Add
dry ingredients all at once, stirring only to moisten dry
ingredients.

Heat shortening or salad oil 3 to 4 inches deep in a heavy
kettle (or deep-fat fryer) to 375 degrees.

Using two soup spoons (dipped in hot fat to keep dough
from sticking), drop dough by rounded spoonfuls into fat,
using second spoon to push dough off first spoon. Fry 3 to 4
minutes to a golden brown. [Most of the doughnuts will turn
themselves over when cooked on one side, but you may have
to give some of them a little help.]

Lift doughnuts from fat with a slotted spoon and drain
on paper towels. Roll hot doughnuts in granulated sugar.

🌱 PUDDING

1 1/4 cups fine dry bread crumbs

2 cups flour

1 cup suet, chopped fine

1 cup raisins

1 cup molasses

1 cup milk

1 tablespoon baking soda

1 teaspoon salt

1 teaspoon cloves

1 teaspoon cinnamon

Combine all ingredients. Pour into a well-oiled 2-quart mold. Cover securely with mold lid or several layers of waxed paper tied in place with string.

Place mold on a rack in a covered container of boiling water. (Water should come halfway up on the mold.) Steam on low heat for 3 hours. Invert pudding onto serving plate.

🌱 LEMON PIE

1 cup sugar

2 tablespoons cornstarch

Juice and grated rind of 1 lemon (2 tablespoons juice;
    1 teaspoon lemon zest)

3 tablespoons butter (about the size of an egg)

1 cup hot water
1 egg, separated
2 tablespoons sugar
1 8-inch pie shell

Combine 1 cup sugar, cornstarch, lemon juice, lemon zest, butter, and hot water in a saucepan. Cook until clear. Remove from heat and put a little of the mixture into a mixing bowl with beaten egg yolk. Stir and return to saucepan; return pan to heat and bring to a boil. Cool.

For meringue, beat egg white until stiff and gradually add 2 tablespoons sugar. Pour filling into a baked shallow 8-inch pie shell. Top with meringue. Bake at 350 degrees for 10 to 15 minutes or until brown.

[Note: The filling needs another tablespoon of cornstarch and another egg yolk to make it thicken. The pie made using the directions above could have been eaten with a straw! It was very sweet and probably could have used twice the lemon juice. Is this perhaps the case of a woman not willing to reveal her pie-making secrets? We hope not!]

Mrs. C. H. Tinkham

Mrs. C. H. Tinkham was a partner with her husband in an early De Smet furniture store. Mrs. Tinkham held the first "dime sociable" in *Little Town on the Prairie*. The Tinkham store was in the same block and across the street from the Ingallses' house in town. Her first recipe reveals the problem with making frosting during that period.

🌱 Cocoa Frosting

4 teaspoons cocoa
2 tablespoons cold water
3 tablespoons hot water
1 teaspoon vanilla
Speck of salt
1 3/4 cups confectioners' sugar

Put cocoa in a saucepan; add cold water and stir until smooth. Add hot water and cook for 1 to 2 minutes; add vanilla and salt. Stir in sugar and beat until smooth and glossy, adding a little more water if too thick or more sugar if too thin.

[Note: To get a frosting thick enough to spread, we used 3 1/2 cups confectioners' sugar, but doing so overpowered the chocolate so that we couldn't taste it. We wouldn't recommend cheating when using an authentic recipe, but frosting right out of a can makes some of these cakes so much more like what you'd expect.]

🌱 Brown Bread

3 cups whole wheat flour
2 cups milk, sweet or sour
1 cup molasses
1/2 cup raisins
2 teaspoons baking soda dissolved in 2 tablespoons boiling water

Combine all ingredients. Pour into four well-greased No. 2 cans. (Cans containing 20 ounces of fruit are usually No. 2 cans.)

Steam for 3 hours. [See instructions for Steam Graham Loaf from Mrs. F. C. Bradley.]

🌿 Baked Bean Soup

1 cup baked beans
1 cup cold water
1 onion
1 cup tomatoes
1 cup milk
1 tablespoon butter
1 tablespoon flour
Salt and pepper to taste
Chopped celery

Cook beans, water, onion, and tomatoes until soft. Strain or puree in food processor. Add milk, butter, and flour to thicken soup. Season to taste with salt and pepper and serve sprinkled with chopped celery.

Mrs. D. W. Wilmarth

The Wilmarths were early settlers of De Smet too. After 1883, they were a prominent part of town life. In company with his brother

George, D. W. ran a grocery that was still in business when old settlers celebrated the fiftieth anniversary of the town. Laura and Almanzo would have known the Wilmarths.

🌿 BLACK CHOCOLATE CAKE

4 (1-ounce) squares unsweetened chocolate
1 cup sour cream, divided
3 eggs, separated
1¼ cups sugar
1 cup flour
1 teaspoon vanilla
1 teaspoon baking soda dissolved in 1 tablespoon
   boiling water

Melt chocolate and ¹/2 cup sour cream. Set aside.

Beat egg yolks, sugar, and remaining ¹/2 cup sour cream. Stir in flour. Add chocolate mixture and vanilla.

Fold in stiffly beaten egg whites. Stir soda mixture into batter.

Pour into a greased and floured 9 x 13-inch baking pan. Bake at 350 degrees for 15 to 20 minutes.

[Note: There is no butter or shortening in this cake! The sour cream supplies the butterfat in this recipe. The batter is rather thick before adding the egg whites, so most of the air is lost when you fold in the whites. This makes a rather thin, fudgy cake. But possibly that was what was intended. This cake was made once using commercial sour cream and again using whipping cream soured with 1 tablespoon lemon juice. Either way, the melted chocolate and sour cream became very thick, making it difficult to completely melt the chocolate without burning the mixture. It might work better to melt the chocolate and then stir in the sour cream.]

❧ CREAM PUFFS

1/2 cup butter
1 cup water
1 cup flour
3 unbeaten eggs

Melt butter in water and bring to a rolling boil. Add flour all at once and stir vigorously until mixture forms a ball that does not separate—30 seconds to 1 minute. Remove from heat and cool for 10 minutes.

Add eggs one at a time, beating about 1 minute or until mixture is smooth again.

Drop dough by rounded tablespoonfuls on a greased baking sheet. Bake at 400 degrees for 20 to 30 minutes until golden brown. Puffs should sound hollow when tapped with a finger. Remove puffs from the baking sheet and cool on a wire rack. When cool, fill with whipped cream.

[Note: Most modern-day recipes for cream puffs recommend using 4 eggs. The additional egg creates more steam in

the baking process, resulting in a cream puff that is hollower
with less eggy dough that needs to be pulled out before
filling the puff.]

❧ PINEAPPLE SHERBET

6 cups water
2 cups sugar
1 (20-ounce) can crushed pineapple, undrained
Juice of 3 lemons (6 tablespoons)
1 egg white (pasteurized)

Simmer water and sugar together to dissolve sugar. Cool.

Puree pineapple in a blender or food processor. [The
authentic alternative is to mash the daylights out of the
pineapple yourself.] Add pineapple and lemon juice to syrup.
Freeze in an ice cream freezer. If using an electric freezer, this
will take about 20 minutes.

Beat egg white. Whisk into sherbet. After serving, freeze
any remaining sherbet.

Mother of Mrs. Neva Whaley Harding

Mrs. Neva Whaley Harding, whose mother's struggle with depression
was discussed earlier in this book, grew up near De Smet and knew the
Ingalls family. Laura and Carrie were significant figures in Mrs. Harding's recollections, which she recorded as part of her one-hundredth
birthday celebration. This is her mother's recipe for strawberry sherbet.

🌿 STRAWBERRY SHERBET

2 cups sugar
4 cups water
2 tablespoons strawberry gelatin (optional)
1 quart strawberries, stems and hulls removed
Juice of 1 lemon (2 tablespoons)
2 egg whites (pasteurized)
2 tablespoons sugar

Simmer 2 cups sugar, water, and gelatin to dissolve sugar.
Cool.

Mash strawberries. Strain by working through a colander
[or puree in a food processor]. Add strawberries to syrup,
along with lemon juice. Freeze in an ice cream freezer. If
using an electric freezer, this will take about 20 minutes.
Frankly, the electric freezer shortcut makes life so much
easier.

Beat egg whites until frothy and gradually add 2 tablespoons sugar. Beat until stiff peaks form. Whisk into the
finished sherbet. After serving, freeze any remaining sherbet.
You can use your modern refrigerator!

And there you have it: real pioneer cookery with all its aches and
pains. Is it any wonder, then, that we have embraced packaged food and
catered church suppers?

The Life of a Prairie Girl

NORTH DAKOTA

MINNESOTA

WISCONSIN

SOUTH DAKOTA

WALNUT GROVE

PEPIN

DE SMET

SPRING VALLEY

BURR OAK

IOWA

NEBRASKA

KANSAS

MISSOURI

INDEPENDENCE

MANSFIELD

MISSISSIPPI RIVER

The Ingalls family in 1894 (left to right): Caroline, Carrie, Laura, Charles, Grace, and Mary

The original "little house in the big woods" no longer exists, but this reproduction log cabin is near Pepin, Wisconsin, where Laura was born. It sits on the land farmed by Pa Ingalls.

When the Ingalls family attempted to homestead near Walnut Grove, Minnesota, they lived in a dugout home like this reproduction, located at the Ingalls Homestead in De Smet, South Dakota. Walnut Grove was the setting for the popular television series *Little House on the Prairie*.

In 1882, Pa Ingalls helped construct the First Congregational Church in De Smet, South Dakota. The building is still in use as a house of worship.

Laura at age 27

Laura and Almanzo's wedding photograph, circa 1885

The prairie land Laura knew so well growing up, as seen now at the Ingalls Homestead, De Smet, South Dakota

Silver Lake, made memorable in Laura's *By the Shores of Silver Lake,* is now just a marsh.

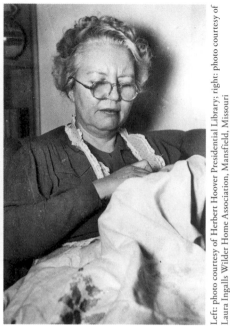

Left: photo courtesy of Herbert Hoover Presidential Library; right: photo courtesy of Laura Ingalls Wilder Home Association, Mansfield, Missouri

Rose Wilder Lane, acclaimed author and daughter who assisted Laura in developing the Little House series, as a youth and later in life

Photo courtesy of Herbert Hoover Presidential Library

Laura and Rose on Tennessee Pass during a road trip through Colorado

The stone cottage that Rose had built for Laura and Almanzo

The Wilder home in Mansfield, Missouri

Laura and Almanzo (with back against left post) visiting on the porch

What Laura Means to Us

Mankind is not following a blind trail; feet were set
upon the true path in the beginning. . . . Let us, with
humble hearts, give thanks for the revelation [given]
to us and our better understanding of the greatness and
goodness of God.

—LAURA INGALLS WILDER

*Y*ou would have thought I might have finished with Mrs. Wilder
and her family when I was a boy. I'd read the entire Little
House series by the end of seventh grade, and youthful enthusiasms
seldom last. However, my discovery of her earlier Ozark writing many
years later in a book called *A Little House Sampler,* edited by William
Anderson, set me going again.

I had worked with a publisher and thought they and fans of Laura
might be interested in the adult columns that Mrs. Wilder did for the
Missouri Ruralist during its heyday. For myself, I was delighted to find,
though from an adult perspective, the same Laura I had come to know
and love from childhood. In fact, I sometimes found the "real" Laura
more interesting than I did the slightly different one from her books.

(As I've pointed out, some incidents in the books are fictional; the family and some other characters are not.)

In fact, my enthusiasm for Laura was such that when I learned my librarian wife had never read the children's books, I sat right down at the kitchen table and read the entire series to her when we spent time in that most homey of rooms. It was there, while I read aloud, that we entered her world where "real things haven't changed. It is still best to be honest and truthful; to make the most of what we have; to be happy with simple pleasures and to be cheerful and have courage when things go wrong," as she wrote in an open letter to the children of Chicago for her eightieth birthday celebration in 1947.

My wife turned out to be *nearly* as fond of the books as I was. She, too, had grown up in a close family and felt the warmth and charm of Laura's story, and she has supported me all the way on my journey of appreciation for all things Laura. Laura's story has the power to draw me along as though I were a hapless magnet being drawn by another. That journey continues and probably will for the rest of my days because things of eternal value are everlastingly fascinating.

For example, while researching this book, I had the good fortune to read Dr. Dale Cockrell's introduction to *The Ingalls Wilder Family Songbook.* While I was reading of how he himself became involved in retelling the Ingallses' pioneering days through referencing and discovering the sources for the songs in the Little House series, I noted that he used the striking phrase the "Great American Family" when discussing the Ingalls family. Although I know Dr. Cockrell, I didn't know he'd written in this vein.

According to him, the idea that there even is such a thing as a great American family is a bit of cultural myth that we, as Americans, have always entertained. All through our storied history, we have looked for examples of what ideal family virtues would look like *if* we ever saw them. His thoughts on the subject really struck me.

I realized that somehow over the years the Ingalls family had come to be that great American family for me. More than any other family I had read about, not excluding the excellent Jo March's family from the novel *Little Women,* I had come to believe that Pa and Ma, Mary, Laura, Carrie, and Grace represent the values we should all cherish and seek to fulfill.

I believe the myth of the great American family is a true myth. Its truth arises because it must. Family is family. The family that prays together stays together. Be it ever so humble, there is no place like home. Keep the home fires burning. Home is where the heart is. And "In love of home, the love of country has its rise," said Charles Dickens in *The Old Curiosity Shop.*

Now, agreed, the Ingallses weren't plaster saints. Laura was honest enough to show her family with its warts in plain view. In the books, she herself is sometimes driven by jealousy over Mary's more attractive hair and ability to get away with bossiness. In one case, she was outraged at something Mary did for which Laura was punished. After being taunted by Mary for having the plainer hair and a snub nose and then being told she must mind Mary because she was the oldest, Laura reached out and slapped her sister. Pa, after Mary ran to him in triumph, heard only one side of the story, and it was Laura who got spanked for both their crimes.

Pa wasn't always a shining example, sometimes getting his way when it would have been better if he'd listened to his wife. He kept on pioneering and moving long after Ma had expressed strong disapproval for not settling down. Pa is also depicted in *By the Shores of Silver Lake* as being good friends with Big Jerry, a horse thief. And Ma can lash out at Pa when the occasion arises, such as when he uses the word *gosh* in *The Long Winter*. To Ma, this was swearing and not to be tolerated!

Doesn't this sound like your family, like my family?

But somehow there is also grace and mercy along the way.

Laura overcame her irritation at Mary's "goodness" and began to strongly admire her character and her acceptance of her blindness. Mary blamed nobody and no divine being for her problems. She was truly thankful for the love of Pa and Ma and God. Ma came to accept her husband's wanderlust, even as he came to accept that he must go no farther and stop in De Smet. There he settled down to be a respected justice of the peace and a bulwark of the Congregational church.

Of course, over the years the little family was separated by different priorities and distance. Laura and Almanzo's move south to the Ozarks was for Almanzo's health, but the rest of the family stayed in South Dakota. Still, they kept in touch, more easily perhaps after Laura started writing for the *Ruralist*. Her sister Carrie remarked, after reading a column, "I do like to have you say kinfolks. It seems to mean so much more than relations or relatives."

We also know from Laura's columns that she and her mother stayed in touch and that the correspondence was precious to Laura. She wrote about receiving a letter from her daughter, Rose, and a letter from her mother and suddenly realizing that she was both mother and daughter herself and that each role had its own reward.

I like to think we can still learn lessons from Laura's accumulated experience and reflection, among which is tolerance for other's failings, courage to start all over again after disaster strikes, and a belief that God holds the future in his hands and intends no ill will for his children.

When Laura and Almanzo were starting their married life, they had a neighbor just across the road from them who frequently borrowed their things but then did not let the Wilders read some of his farm newspapers that contained advice that might have helped them. He never loaned out his papers, he said. He was simply exasperating that way, but he turned out to be a good neighbor when Almanzo and Laura were sick. Mr. Skelton, as she called him, was so humorous I can't resist quoting Laura:

> Mr. Skelton was a good borrower but a very poor hand to return anything. . . . He borrowed the hand tools and the farm machinery, the grindstone and the whetstone, and the harness and saddles, also groceries and kitchen tools.
>
> One day he came over and borrowed my wash boiler in which to heat water for butchering. In a few minutes he returned, and making a separate trip for each article, he borrowed both my dishpans, my two butcher knives, the knife sharpener, a couple of buckets, the boards on which to lay the hog, some matches to light his fire, and as an afterthought while the water was heating, he came for some salt. There was a fat hog in our pen, and I half expected him to come back once more and borrow the hog, but luckily he had a hog of his own.

And yet Laura admitted, "This family were kind neighbors later when we really needed their help."

Pioneering was a constant lesson in learning how to put up with the foibles of others.

Pioneering was also a constant lesson in learning how to put things behind you and start all over again. The great expansion westward saw hopeful wanderers take claims, take out loans, fail on the loans, and then move on and try again. Because of confusion arising from the

Little House narrative itself and Pa's actual biography, we get different numbers, but it appears Pa Ingalls made at least five or six tries before settling near De Smet. In reality, there were moves to Kansas, back to the Big Woods in Wisconsin, from the Big Woods to Minnesota, a retreat to Iowa, a move again back to Minnesota, and finally a move to De Smet. Laura's books could have been written as a tragedy, but they weren't because, at heart, Laura retained her trusting faith in God. The future is always better further on, or so she felt.

After the searing trauma of losing her hundred-dollar bill upon her and Almanzo's arrival in Mansfield, they recovered that bill, and that was their turning point. They initially purchased a few acres, and the farm eventually grew to two hundred acres in size. Quite a property for the Ozarks.

They lived on a hilltop and over time acquired gravity-fed running water, electricity, and, though they never sought it, world fame. Laura launched into her Methodist church activities and there was no turning back. She wrote, "There is no elation equal to the rise of the spirit to meet and overcome a difficulty . . . by praying, now and then, the prayer of a good fighter . . . : 'Lord, make me sufficient to mine own occasion.'"

On February 10, 1957, Mrs. Wilder, famed author and pioneer, passed away at the age of ninety. Near her was her family reference Bible with a list of favorite verses. One of them, Romans 8:35, 37–39, reads,

Who shall separate us from the love of Christ? shall tribulation, or distress, or persecution, or famine, or nakedness, or peril, or sword? . . . Nay, in all these things we are more than conquerors through him that loved us. For I am persuaded, that neither death, nor life, nor angels, nor principalities, nor powers, nor

things present, nor things to come, nor height, nor depth, nor
any other creature, shall be able to separate us from the love of
God, which is in Christ Jesus our Lord.

Her long journey was at an end, leaving a spiritual legacy we all can
treasure.

Appendix I: Remembering the De Smet of Old

In 1939 the Wilders returned to De Smet to attend the Old Settlers Day Celebration marking the founding of the town, the very town for which Pa Ingalls was credited as being the first settler during the "hard winter" of 1880–81. What gave Laura and Almanzo, then seventy-three and eighty-two, the courage to embark on such a trip when the roads were rugged and poorly marked, I don't know, but nevertheless they ventured out and, in fact, got lost three times on the first day of their journey.

Mrs. Wilder wrote in an article for the *Christian Science Monitor* that the De Smet celebration was the highlight of her and Almanzo's trip. Yet, for all the highlights of the trip, it was something of a melancholy journey too. Cap Garland, a prominent character in the children's books, had died. This brave young fellow, who had gone with Almanzo to buy seed wheat from a farmer and save the town from starvation during the hard winter, had been killed in a steam thresher explosion. Farm accidents were a way of life back then and among the trials the settlers had to endure.

All of Almanzo's family had moved away from De Smet. Royal left to keep store in Minnesota, and Eliza Jane Wilder, the teacher Laura had such a conflict with in *Little Town on the Prairie,* had also given up her claim and eventually moved south to warmer climes. If only the pioneers had had the benefit of modern weather science, they would have understood the severity of the climate where they were trying to farm!

But there was no National Weather Service to warn them that—despite what railroad advertising told them—they were moving into essentially parched country, not well suited for traditional crops. What the settlers called a drought was really the normal weather pattern of the Dakotas returning after a period of unusually high rainfall had ceased. But it took years of many settlers going broke for the nature of the climate to be understood.

As it was, during their visit, the town of De Smet was very different from what Laura and Almanzo remembered:

The little town we used to know was gone. In its place was a town that spread North beyond the railroad tracks, East to the lake shore, South where the big slough used to be and far to the West. The old schoolhouse was gone. Its place was taken by a large brick school building.

Along Main street were fine business houses in place of the one story with a two story false front, stores of the old days.

A large brick bank with offices above stood on the corner where Pa had built his small office building. We took rooms in a hotel a little way from it.

Next morning at breakfast, two men looked sharply at us as they passed our table, then came back and stopped.

"Hello, Laura," one of them said.

I looked up in surprise into the laughing black eyes of a tall man.

"I am Laura, but who are you?" I answered him.

"I am Sam," he said, "I would know you anywhere." And then I remembered him for an old schoolmate, one of the younger boys in our crowd.

As they visited, even more memories came rushing back. Pa and his family had not only been among the town's first citizens but had also largely populated the first church, the very first service having taken place in their home, as recorded in the town newspaper.

A fiftieth anniversary celebration of the founding of the "little town on the prairie," held in June 1930, was superintended by a committee and the De Smet newspaper. Laura and Almanzo were not able to attend, but Laura waxed poetical at the thought of the return of so many old settlers from fifty years ago, and she called to mind, with nostalgia, what she remembered of the beauty of the land. She wrote this poem, published in the newspaper, for the occasion.

Dakota Prairies

Ever I see them in my mental vision
As first my eyes beheld them years agone;
Clad all in brown with russet shades and golden
Stretching away into the far unknown;
Never a break to mar their sweep of grandeur;
From North to South, from East to West the same,
Save that the East was full of purple shadows,
The West with setting sun was all aflame;
Never a sign of human habitation
To show that man's domain was begun;
The only marks the footpaths of the bison

Made by the herds before their day was done.

The sky downturned a brazen bowl to me,

And clanging with the calls of wild gray geese

Winging their way unto the distant Southland

To 'scape the coming storms and rest in peace.

Ever the winds went whispering o'er the prairies,

Ever the grasses whispered back again,

And then the sun dipped down below the skyline,

And stars lit just the outline of the plain.

Carter P. Sherwood was the distinguished editor of the paper, and he and his son, Aubrey, ran the *News* a combined ninety-some years. Carter was a keen local historian, as was his son. In fact, when Aubrey later took over the paper from his father, he became the town historian and corresponded frequently with Laura, who helped him clarify reminiscences from the early days when the town seemed to spring up overnight on the prairie. The following records are gathered from their newspaper variously named the *De Smet Leader* and, later, the *De Smet News*. Much firsthand information on the Ingallses' church-founding activities can be gleaned from the paper's archives.

Ingalls Was First Resident De Smet: Family of R. R. Timekeeper Lived at Silver Lake in 1879; Moved to Town

A railroad timekeeper and clerk came to be the first resident of De Smet, and remained to take an active part in its development, he and his family making it their home through the remainder of the lives of the parents. This man was C. P. Ingalls.

In giving credit to those who took part in the pioneering of Kingsbury county and De Smet, Mr. Ingalls has the honor of being the first in several distinctions. He was the first resident, first to have a family with him here, quite possibly first to establish a home on the townsite, first justice of the peace and first town clerk.

Mr. and Mrs. Ingalls and their family drove from Tracy, Minn., the end of the railroad, to where Brookings is now located, the husband and father being engaged as bookkeeper and timekeeper at the construction camp. This was early in 1879, and in the late summer, as construction moved west, they drove from Brookings to the camp on the banks of Silver Lake, then a pretty little body of water and the resting place for all kinds of wild water birds—ducks, swans, geese and pelicans.

In the Ingalls family there were: Mary, who died two years ago, Laura (Mrs. Manley Wilder), Mansfield, Mo., Grace (Mrs. Nate Dow), of Manchester, and Carrie (Mrs. D. N. Swanzey of Keystone).

Mrs. Swanzey recalls that the camp was a busy place, with many drivers and teams who returned to camp at night with clouds of dust, shouts of drivers and galloping horses. That was the signal for the children to run in for supper and bed. Meanwhile the men showed rivalry over their teams and their knowledge of how to handle a scraper. There were some good horses in that camp and Mrs. Swanzey says it is no wonder that occasionally a thief would pick out a good horse, and when there had been visitors about during the day the men would sleep by their horses that night.

In the fall the camp broke up, the surveyors and graders

went back East, and the Ingalls family moved into the cabin that the engineers had built, Mr. Ingalls to spend the winter looking after things for the railroad company. They bought the food supply left at the company camp, this including some hardtack.

The winter of 1879–80 was a very mild one, and Mrs. Wilder, writing from Mansfield, Mo., to tell of those early days, reports that about Christmas time Mr. and Mrs. R. A. Boast arrived and lived in a little house within a few steps of the Ingalls. [*sic*] It was in that house that the Boasts entertained "the whole of De Smet and Lake Preston" on New Year's Day.

The two towns—neither of them yet in existence—were represented on that day by the Ingalls family and a bachelor named Walter Ogden, who lived near the site of Lake Preston. Mr. Boast always described the day as a warm one—so mild that the doors were left open.

The Ingalls home was a stopping place for the early home-seekers, and they played host as best they could, their house being practically a hotel that first year. It was also the scene of the first religious service and the family played an important part in the early religious history of the community, described in another article in this paper.

Mrs. Swanzey describes the bird life of that first spring as the children recall it: "As it got warmer the wild ducks and geese began to come. Early one morning there was such a noise that we ran out of doors, to find the lake covered with wild geese, swimming and splashing—every goose talking. Our parents told us that they were choosing their mates, as it was St. Valentine's Day. Mornings we would watch the lake, and with the wind blowing the water in little waves and with wild ducks and geese and occasionally swans, it was a sight no child could forget."

Mrs. Swanzey continues: "Spring came, and with it the surveyors. Father used to go with them and one day he came home and said the town was all located. After dinner I went to the top of the hill, east of where the court house now is, to see the town, and all I saw was a lot of stakes in the ground. I went back and told Mother there was nothing but a lot of sticks stuck in the ground and she told me that where they were would be houses, stores, a schoolhouse and a church."

Relieved of his railroad caretaker job Mr. Ingalls moved to town, building a small place where the Penny store now is, later selling it to E. H. Couse for a hardware store. He then built a small place diagonally across the corner and there the family lived. Mr. Ingalls was one of the first justices of the peace of the county and the first justice court was held in the front room of this small house. Church services were held there, too.

(Editor's note: From the official minutes of 1880 we read that E. W. Smith was appointed justice in April but moved away in May and Mr. Ingalls succeeded him.)

In her letter about the early history Mrs. Wilder tells of her husband's location on his homestead in 1879, but states that he went back to "civilization" for the winter and they did not meet until some time later. He spent the winter of 1880–81 in De Smet, as did the Ingalls family.

Mrs. Swanzey closes her letter: "Details slip my memory but impressions last, and the lives of the early pioneers were bound together in an effort to build for the future, not only a town but a good town. There are others who can tell you better of the Hard Winter, of grinding wheat in coffee mills for flour, of the snow and drifts and the spirit of comradeship in the little town."

The Ingalls family were to move later to their farm southeast of town and live there some years. Later they lived in De Smet on Third street, both parents passing away here.

De Smet's Pioneer Church Is Celebrating Fiftieth Anniversary This Year, Too

Churches played an early part in the development of Kingsbury county and of De Smet vicinity, this year of 1930 being the fiftieth anniversary of the organization of the first church at the county seat.

The church record of the earliest days seems to be lost. Notes left by Mrs. C. P. Ingalls, first residents, have been valuable to the church clerk, who has prepared this history.

The first church was named The First Congregational Church of De Smet, and the organization came fifty years ago this month, June 20, 1880. . . .

The first religious service in the community was held in the Ingalls home near Silver Lake on February 29, 1880. The Rev. E. H. Alden, working under the Rev. Stewart Sheldon, Congregational missionary superintendent for Dakota Territory, held this meeting. Mr. Alden was given a commission to supply this field for the first six months of 1880. Among those present at this first service were Mr. and Mrs. C. P. Ingalls, Mary, Laura, Carrie and Grace, Mr. and Mrs. R. A. Boast, T. H. Ruth, A. W.

Ogden, Mr. O'Connell and William O'Connell, and others, making twenty-five in all.

The missionary went on west but returned for later services held in this house until May, when the depot was partly completed and they were held there, the agent, Rev. H. G. Woodworth, holding them part of the time.

In May Mr. Alden relinquished the field to the Rev. Edward Brown, and it was he who on June 20, 1880, at a meeting in the still unfinished depot, organized the First Congregational Church of De Smet. The membership was Mr. and Mrs. C. P. Ingalls and Mary, the Rev. and Mrs. Edward Brown, Mr. and Mrs. S. N. Gilbert and V. V. Barnes, all joining by letter from other churches. Mr. Barnes was chosen as clerk.

The next record Mr. Mallery finds is of the October sixth meeting, when the articles of incorporation were drawn and signed by Mr. Barnes, Mr. Brown, S. C. Sherwin, C. L. [Caroline Lake] Ingalls, Orville Sherwin, Mary Ingalls and C. P. Ingalls. Under this organization a regular meeting was held at three p.m., October 9, 1880, at the home of Mr. Barnes, and he, Mr. Ingalls and S. N. Gilbert were elected trustees. The articles of incorporation were sent to Yankton and filed, and on November 10, 1880, a Certificate of Corporate Existence was granted to the church by the secretary of the territory.

A Commitment to Get Things Going

The people of De Smet weren't the sort of folk to sit around and hope someone else would assist them in starting religious services. They were rough and ready in the West and willing to start on their own. And this meant getting started with very little funding. First religious services took place in houses or at the railroad depot, where the stationmaster himself was a minister of sorts. *By the Shores of Silver Lake* mentions these types of early services.

Congregationalists were aggressive in moving west, and the Congregational Church Building Society offered a $500 loan to start a church building if it could be matched by the community. That was in 1881. Only $200 was raised by the locals—still a huge sum—but the church went ahead with building anyway in 1882. No sense wasting time; they could live by faith.

There was a great spirit of ecumenism in those days, and the Congregationalists generously shared their building with the Methodists and the Baptists until they could build their own houses of worship. Once they did, Episcopal services were sometimes held at the Baptist church. And when the Catholic church burned down, it received help and the offer of a meeting place from other churches in town. "Union" services were also held from time to time so that all who might wish to worship together could do so.

Though money remained scarce, the Congregationalists were duly proud to add a church bell to their building in 1884 for a cost of about $100. This no doubt took some faith giving as well. But the amount of sharing across party lines is to be noted. This made scarce funds go further and advanced all types of believers.

This excerpt from the *Kingsbury County News* of August 30, 1883, reprinted later by Aubrey Sherwood, shows the early ecumenical attitude of the pioneers:

CHURCHES—Congregational, Rev. E. Brown, pastor, services every Sabbath 10:30 a.m. and 7:30 p.m., alternating

with Methodist Church once in four weeks. Methodist, Rev. P.
L. Hooker, pastor, services at church once in four weeks at
10:30, once in Holy Week, the intermediate weeks at 7:30 p.m.
Catholic, Rev. Thomas O'Riley, pastor, services at the schoolhouse every fourth Sunday at 10:30 a.m. Baptist, Rev. G. N.
Annis, pastor, services at the Congregational Church every other
Sunday at 2 p.m. Union Sunday School every Sunday at 12
o'clock noon. Union Prayer Meeting—every Wednesday
evening at 7 o'clock.

Appendix 2: An Interview with Laura's Friend Neta Seal

Perhaps Laura's best friend over the last two decades of her life was a woman named Neta Seal. Her husband, Silas, owned a service station and garage in Mansfield. Neta helped her husband there and also rented out apartments and sometimes took in laundry. Her perspective is one of the best on Laura's habits and manner of life.

I interviewed Neta when she was in her eighties. Her memory was clear, and a picture of Laura in her "retirement" would not be complete without Neta's recollections of what Mrs. Wilder was like at that time—after she had become a celebrity because of her books, which she was still working on in the late 1930s when Neta and Laura first met.

When I say retirement with regard to Laura, I mean from farming. I'm not sure Mrs. Wilder really retired until Almanzo died in 1949. It was about that time when Irene Lichty, who was to become the first curator of what is now called the Laura Ingalls Wilder Historic Home and Museum in Mansfield, began taking Laura to church again, after an absence because of Almanzo's illness. Another friend, Mrs. Iola Jones, also drove Laura to church.

Neta and Laura's becoming acquainted was important for the purposes of fellowship and friendship—and for a bit of rest and relaxation.

A writer's life is lonely, and Laura still had about eight years to put in on her Little House series before she was clear of that labor in 1945. Neta provided a diversion from ever-present work. Here's part of my interview with her:

How we met the Wilders is sort of a long story. We came back from Detroit and bought a filling station, or a service station, we called it then, because it was all service.

One morning Almanzo came in and my husband checked his tires and cleaned his windshield and his windows and said, with a smile, "Mr. Wilder, what will you have?"

"Seal, you don't know whether I'm going to buy a dime's worth of gas from you," Mr. Wilder said, "but you give me all this free service, then ask me what I want."

"Well, Mr. Wilder you need your windshield cleaned, and you need the right amount of air in your tires, if you are going to drive," my husband replied. And that made a friend.

Mr. Wilder was always in there after that. He'd come into the service station and let Mrs. Wilder out—he called her Bessie and she called him Manly—to go to the grocery store, to the bank, or whatever she wanted to do. It was the kind of place where people gathered to talk. We sold gas and oil and all those things, and folks would just come down. I would say that Mrs. Wilder was the more outgoing and had a pretty good sense of humor.

By the time we got acquainted with them both, Mr. Wilder was crippled and used a cane. He walked with a limp and had one club foot. His shoe had to have a real thick sole. . . .

Almanzo didn't have horses anymore; he had sold them.

But he did have some goats. I can't remember exactly how many he had, maybe four or five, maybe six. He didn't have a big herd of them. These were milk goats, and he milked them by hand. He had a barn, and he had a little stand for them to step up on, and he'd go out there, and they'd come and jump up on it. He'd sit down and milk one; then he would turn that one out and let the next one in. But finally he got to where he couldn't take care of them so he sold them.

They always had a dog up till old Ben died. He was a bulldog. They always had bulldogs after I got acquainted with them. . . .

Here's a funny little story about the dog. He had a boil on his jaw; and when it went to hurting him so bad, he'd come in and lay his head in her lap and look up as if he was saying, "Can you do anything for me?" Then she would get some salve and rub it on his jaw. When that was done, he would go back and lay down. Finally, it was healed.

Mrs. Wilder—I always called her Mrs. Wilder—didn't even have a dog after he [Almanzo] went away.

Going West with the Wilders

You know, I did meet some of her family. We had come back from Detroit and had bought the filling station, but they were going to have to work on the streets, pave them or something. We didn't have anything to do, but Mr. Wilder wanted my husband to drive them on a trip to California.

So my husband came in one day and asked me if I would like a trip to California with the Wilders. I hesitated a minute, then replied: "I don't know them well enough to make a long trip with them."

"Now is a good time to become acquainted. All it will cost us is money for our meals and lodging." *You could get cabins for fifty cents a night then* [italics added].

We left Mansfield early in May and got back by the end of the month.

Singing with Mrs. Wilder

On the trip we sang little crazy songs, Mrs. Wilder and I did, in the back seat, just to pass the time away:

Waltz me around, O Willy,
Around and around and around.
And I'll give you some kisses
To make up for misses,
So waltz me around and around.

She loved that one because it was kind of fast. We'd just sing it over and over. Another one was "She Drives a Cadillac":

She drives a Cadillac;
I walk to work and back.
Oh boy, that's where my money goes.
My money goes
To buy my baby clothes.
(I buy her everything
For to keep her in style.)

She drives a little red Ford;
I ride the running board.
Oh boy, that's where my money goes.

While on our journey, Mr. Wilder was collecting branches
to make walking canes. He really wanted a cane from each state
in the Union. During a stop, he saw a tree he wanted a branch
from for a cane. My husband cut the branch from the tree,
and as they drove away, they came upon this sign: "This Park
Protected by Law." They were certainly happy they hadn't been
caught.

Mrs. Wilder tried to find a native Californian, but it
seemed that everyone she talked to were natives of other states.
One day we were sightseeing when Mrs. Wilder called excitedly,
"I've found a native!" The man knew their daughter, Rose
Wilder Lane, so they had a delightful visit with him.

Yes, it was quite a trip because we came back by way of the
Black Hills of South Dakota. Laura's sister Carrie was living
there in Keystone right by Mt. Rushmore. So we got us a cabin,
and they stayed with Carrie [Carrie had married a widowed
miner named David Swanzey].

She was about the same size as Laura, small, and she was
really nice. A year or two after this visit, Carrie came down
to Mansfield to visit, and we were with them quite a while
because we would take them driving to see different parts of
the Ozarks.

Carrie's husband wasn't with her; he had died.

Laura's sister Grace was also still living over at De Smet.
Grace was taller than either Laura or Carrie, as I remember. She

was built more like Rose, but she was a little plump, not fat. I
don't remember Grace visiting the Wilders in Mansfield while
I knew them.

When we took that trip, I think Mrs. Wilder had finished
her books. Maybe not all of them. But she had done most of the
writing. I got autographed copies of all of them. She gave me the
full set with the statement: "You're not to loan these to anybody.
If they want to read them they can go to the library or buy
them. Because if you start loaning them out they'll be torn up,
and they'll be lost and you won't have them." So I never loaned
them.

We weren't members of any of the same clubs, but after that
trip we were fast friends. I was a Baptist and she was a Methodist, and I didn't attend a lot of clubs. They were both pretty
much retired when we knew them. And they did have a modern
farmhouse. Water was piped up to the house from a little ravine
in back that had a spring. They also had indoor plumbing and a
bathroom, though they didn't use modern heat. It was propane.
We don't have natural gas down here even now.

Mr. Wilder

In his retirement, Mr. Wilder had a shop that kept him busy.
He'd go putter in that shop. Now we built an apartment house,
and we lived in part of it and rented the other part—just two
rooms—and Mr. Wilder got it in his head that he wanted to
move into one of them apartments.

Mrs. Wilder told me, "He just pesters me to death to move
into one of them apartments." So she said, "One day I told him,

I said, 'Now, Manly, you go out to your workshop; we can't take that with us, you know. You'll have to sort it out and sell it. Now you go out there and make a list of anything you're going to sell before we move in.'"

He went out there and was gone quite a while. When he came back, he never said another word about moving from that time until he died. He didn't want to get rid of his workshop.

Mr. Wilder could make beautiful furniture. He once gave us a table that was made out of a cypress tree he brought back from Florida. It's back in their old home now. We let the home have it because it would mean a lot to the public to see that. And then he gave us a big, wide-armed chair he made out of sassafras. We left that in the home too, just like it was when they lived there.

I don't know whatever happened to the apple orchard. [Almanzo grew apples during the early years of his Ozark farming.] It's all gone. I imagine it just rotted. After we got to know them, they sold the biggest part of their farm to the Shorters. It was just too much for him to look after. They made payments to Mr. Wilder rather than pay full price because he said, "I want some income. I'll let him pay it out in payments each month and then I'll have some money."

The Final Years

[Note: When Almanzo died, Laura was at a loss. She was still pretty healthy for a time, before diabetes finally caught up with her, but she could sew, crochet, and embroider, all things her mother would have done in her declining years. What she couldn't do was get around as much, so her remaining friends pitched in to help her.]

We went out there every Sunday afternoon to see her. We'd take her for drives. For a while she owned a Chrysler, I think, then she sold it.

There was a man by the name of Mr. Hartley here in town who was a taxi driver. So she finally let him go get her and bring her to town for the groceries. I had always done that and taken her to the bank, but I had this apartment house with four sleeping rooms I rented by night. It got to be too much work, so she let him drive her. Helen Burkhiser did a book on me [*Neta, Laura's Friend*] that exhausted me when I saw what all I had done.

Mrs. Wilder passed her time by doing a lot of reading, I think. [She kept her Bible open on the kitchen table.] That was until her eyes failed. She did like to keep the radio on, but I don't remember what she listened to. I don't remember there ever being any TV.

I don't remember as good as I used to. For example, I don't remember any of her favorite foods except that both her and Almanzo especially liked my Swiss steak. And I don't remember her saying that she had a favorite of her own books, but she did talk about her family, the whole family, but more about her sisters Mary and Grace.

Oh, Mrs. Wilder did get letters from school children, letters and letters and letters. At first, she answered each one individually, but then her eyes began to fail her. She had diabetes, and that's what caused it. Anyway, she got to where she'd just write the teacher a letter and let her read it to all the children. She even got letters from Japan.

Since then many Japanese have come to Mansfield to visit the home. One summer [1991] they even made a movie of this place, took a helicopter and flew it all over the little town of Mansfield. They took pictures at the farm and at the school.

Mrs. Wilder and her daughter, Rose, stayed in close touch, both by telephone and by letter. I don't think Rose made it to her father's funeral. [This was odd because she had a sympathetic relationship with her father and a more contentious relationship with her mother.] She did come down before her mother's final illness, while Mrs. Wilder was in the Springfield hospital.

One of the things we did while she was in the hospital was to take Mrs. Wilder water out of her own well. We would take her jugs of water every time we went to see her. She didn't like the Springfield water.

Mrs. Wilder was able to come home from the hospital to the house she and Mr. Wilder had built together. Not much later she died there in the home [February 10, 1957].

Acknowledgments

My appreciation for help in the making of *A Prairie Girl's Faith* goes out to the following persons and entities:

To the South Dakota Historical Society Press and to director Nancy Koupal, thanks for permission to quote from the best-selling *Pioneer Girl: The Annotated Autobiography,* and to Jennifer McIntyre for her help in the process.

To librarians and personnel at the Nashville Public Library, the Brentwood Public Library, and the Williamson County Public Library, thanks for assistance and cooperation.

To Lynn Smith, audiovisual archivist for the Herbert Hoover Presidential Library, thanks for information on the use of photographs from their collection.

To the *De Smet News* and to publisher Dale Blegen, thanks for help and information on former publisher Aubrey Sherwood.

To the *Missouri Ruralist* staff, thanks for providing guidance many years ago as to the extent of Mrs. A. J. Wilder's columns that ran from 1911 through 1924 and began her career.

To the University of Missouri Press, thanks for a willingness to publish *Laura Ingalls Wilder, Farm Journalist,* a complete collection of Mrs. Wilder's columns in the paper that gave her a real start in journalism and creative writing.

To Tessa Flak, director of the Laura Ingalls Wilder Memorial Society, thanks for direction in the use of Pa's obituary from their website.

To Larry Dennis, publisher of the *Mansfield Mirror,* thanks for helping me find useful and rare photographs for my book.

To Robin L. Cuany, father-in-law, thanks for photographs taken while on vacation in De Smet, South Dakota.

To Jean Coday, director of the Laura Ingalls Wilder Historic Home and Museum, and to her staff, thanks for granting permission to use photographs from their collection.

To Jane Hines, beloved sister, who kitchen-tested recipes in the chapter "The Church Potluck," thanks for taking the time to modernize the measurements while leaving the recipes authentic.

To Gwendolyn Hines, wife and retired librarian at John Overton High School, Nashville, Tennessee, thanks for many editorial suggestions and corrections to the text of this book.

To Megan Hines, daughter, thanks for help in proofreading and editing the manuscript.

To Bruce Nygren, senior editor, and Kathy Mosier, production editor, at WaterBrook, thanks for guiding the manuscript to a successful completion.

Notes

Introduction

1 *As a child I learned my Bible lessons by heart:* Quoted in Stephen W. Hines, ed., *Laura Ingalls Wilder, Farm Journalist: Writings from the Ozarks* (Columbia: University of Missouri Press, 2007), 236.

1 *We called it buffalo grass:* A personal memory corrected by research: Scott Vogt, "Buffalograss: Five Keys to a Successful Planting," Dyck Arboretum of the Plains, June 3, 2015, http://dyckarboretum.org/buffalograss-five-keys-successful-planting/.

2 *from her personal point of view:* Pamela Smith Hill, *Laura Ingalls Wilder: A Writer's Life* (Pierre: South Dakota State Historical Society Press, 2007), 136–37.

3 *I am a descendant of pioneers myself:* Information from the Sullivan County, Indiana, courthouse archive, family history section.

Chapter 1: Pioneer Faith

5 *There is no turning back:* Quoted in Stephen W. Hines, ed., *Laura Ingalls Wilder, Farm Journalist: Writings from the Ozarks* (Columbia: University of Missouri Press, 2007), 255.

6 *Dr. John E. Miller . . . has noted their journey:* John E. Miller, *Becoming Laura Ingalls Wilder: The Woman Behind the Legend* (Columbia: University of Missouri Press, 1998), 16–17.

6   *considered themselves in the mainstream of Protestantism:*
Miller, *Becoming Laura Ingalls Wilder,* 15–16.

8   *warned of the dangers of licking icicles:* Laura Ingalls Wilder,
Pioneer Girl: The Annotated Autobiography, ed. Pamela Smith
Hill (Pierre: South Dakota Historical Society Press, 2014),
61–62.

8   *It was such a comfort to tell her:* Wilder, *Pioneer Girl,* 62.

9   *The "now I lay me down to sleep" prayers:* Laura Ingalls
Wilder, *Little House in the Big Woods* (1932; repr., New York:
HarperTrophy, 1971), 115.

12   *there are at least 126 songs:* Dale Cockrell, ed., *The Happy
Land Companion* (Nashville: NDX Press, 2005), v.

12   *There's a land that is fairer than day:* Sanford Fillmore Bennett, "Sweet By and By," in Cockrell, *Happy Land Companion,*
39–40.

13   *tells of a weary traveler:* Narration by Mose Case, 1863;
performed by Riders in the Sky, "The Arkansas Traveler," *The
Arkansas Traveler: Music from Little House on the Prairie,*
produced by Butch Baldassari and Dale Cockrell, Cackle &
Splash Music, 2006.

13   *"Captain Jinks":* Cockrell, *Happy Land Companion,* 10–13.

Chapter 2: Still Looking for the Promised Land

15   *Laura could not say what she meant:* Laura Ingalls Wilder,
These Happy Golden Years (1943; repr., New York: Harper
Trophy, 1971), 153.

16   *Astonishingly Pa was able to obtain:* John E. Miller, *Becoming
Laura Ingalls Wilder: The Woman Behind the Legend* (Columbia, MO: University of Missouri Press, 1998), 32.

17 *Pa, as one of the founding members:* Sallie Ketcham, *Laura Ingalls Wilder: American Writer on the Prairie* (New York: Routledge, 2015), 32.

18 *All that winter we all went to our church:* Laura Ingalls Wilder, *Pioneer Girl: The Annotated Autobiography,* ed. Pamela Smith Hill (Pierre: South Dakota Historical Society Press, 2014), 136.

22 *job as a clerk at the Masters Hotel:* Miller, *Becoming Laura Ingalls Wilder,* 36–37.

24 *chills would run up and down her spine:* Laura Ingalls Wilder, *Little Town on the Prairie* (1941; repr., New York: Harper-Trophy, 1971), 277.

25 *Charles's sister Ladocia offered an opportunity to him:* Miller, *Becoming Laura Ingalls Wilder,* 44.

26 *by letter from other churches:* "De Smet's Pioneer Church Is Celebrating Fiftieth Anniversary This Year, Too," *De Smet News,* June 6, 1930.

27 *This was my first school:* Stephen W. Hines, ed., *Little House in the Ozarks: The Rediscovered Writings* (Nashville: Thomas Nelson, 1991), 169–170.

29 *Laura was called Bessie:* William Holtz, *The Ghost in the Little House: A Life of Rose Wilder Lane* (Columbia: University of Missouri Press, 1993), 41.

31 *the hundred-dollar bill was missing:* Laura Ingalls Wilder, *On the Way Home* (1962; repr., New York: HarperTrophy, 1976), 79–83.

Chapter 3: Partners in Faith

33 *Lay not up for yourselves treasures upon earth:* Quoted by Laura Ingalls Wilder in an October 1920 *Missouri Ruralist* column.

33 *once commented that Almanzo:* Stephen W. Hines, *"I Remember Laura"* (Nashville: Thomas Nelson, 1994), 224.

34 *a regular part of their lives:* Pamela Smith Hill, *Laura Ingalls Wilder: A Writer's Life* (Pierre: South Dakota State Historical Society Press, 2007), 89.

34 *Sunday was also the most boring day of the week:* Laura Ingalls Wilder, *Farmer Boy* (1933; repr., New York: HarperTrophy, 1971), 94.

34 *eating and drinking:* Matthew 11:19.

34 *that is the first time Laura realizes she has a beau:* Laura Ingalls Wilder, *Little Town on the Prairie* (1941; repr., New York: HarperTrophy, 1971), 278–82.

35 *He himself was a homesteader:* Laura Ingalls Wilder, *Pioneer Girl: The Annotated Autobiography,* ed. Pamela Smith Hill (Pierre: South Dakota Historical Society Press, 2014), 194.

35 *Mark had a stake in the local newspaper:* Aubrey Sherwood, *Beginnings of De Smet* (De Smet, SD: Aubrey Sherwood, 1979), 24.

36 *became active in the Methodist church there:* John E. Miller, *Laura Ingalls Wilder and Rose Wilder Lane: Authorship, Place, Time, and Culture* (Columbia: University of Missouri Press, 2008), 52.

36 *Historian William Anderson noted that the church was already organized:* William Anderson, ed., *A Little House Reader* (New York: HarperCollins, 1998), 113–14.

37 *Just such a teacher was Mr. A. C. Barton:* Stephen Hines, ed., *Saving Graces: The Inspirational Writings of Laura Ingalls Wilder* (Nashville: Broadman & Holman, 1997), 145–48.

38   *Laura could speak approvingly of the practice of washing one another's feet:* Anderson, *A Little House Reader,* 114–17.

38   *In the chapter "Barnum Walks":* Laura Ingalls Wilder, *These Happy Golden Years* (1943; repr., New York: HarperTrophy, 1971), 213.

Chapter 4: Shadows on the Grass

39   *We are told that the life of a woman on a farm:* Quoted in Stephen W. Hines, ed., *Laura Ingalls Wilder, Farm Journalist: Writings from the Ozarks* (Columbia: University of Missouri Press, 2007), 50.

41   *purchased the* Missouri Ruralist: Pamela Smith Hill, *Laura Ingalls Wilder: A Writer's Life* (Pierre, SD: South Dakota State Historical Society Press, 2007), 61.

41   *The whole world was a deep, dark blue:* Stephen W. Hines, ed., *Little House in the Ozarks: The Rediscovered Writings* (Nashville: Thomas Nelson, 1991), 138.

41   *the fullest, finest and most powerful novel:* "Ole Edvart Rölvaag," *Encyclopedia of World Biography,* Detroit, MI: Gale, 1998, http://link.galegroup.com/apps/doc/K1631005652 /SUIC?u=tel_s_tsla&xid=38b7d930.

41   *the most penetrating and mature depictment:* Henry Steele Commager, "The Literature of the Pioneer West," *Minnesota History* 8, no. 4 (December 1927): 319, 325–26.

43   *During the hard winter of 1880–81 . . . the whole Whaley family:* Neva Harding, *I Recall Pioneer Days in South Dakota* (Brookings, SD: The Woman's Club and The Saturday Literary Club, 1972), 3.

43   *the same tunes that Pa played:* Harding, *I Recall Pioneer Days in South Dakota,* 3.

45   *she worked on the farm around the clock:* Harding, *I Recall Pioneer Days in South Dakota,* 9–10.

45   *Mother's lot was to stay home all day:* Harding, *I Recall Pioneer Days in South Dakota,* 9–10.

47   *The book was derived right from the history of Mama Bess:* Hill, *Laura Ingalls Wilder,* 149–52.

47   *canst not then be false to any man:* William Shakespeare, *Hamlet,* act 1, scene 3, line 566.

48   *In the fell clutch of circumstance:* W. E. Henley, "Invictus," in *Adventures in Reading,* ed. Evan Lodge and Marjorie Braymer (New York: Harcourt, Brace: 1958), 209.

48   *But presently my mind took a wider range:* Hines, ed., *Little House in the Ozarks,* 138–39.

49   *Things and persons appear to us:* Hines, ed., *Little House in the Ozarks,* 225.

Chapter 5: A Mary and Martha Mix

51   *Oh, for a little time to enjoy the beauties around me:* Quoted in Stephen W. Hines, ed., *Laura Ingalls Wilder, Farm Journalist: Writings from the Ozarks* (Columbia: University of Missouri Press, 2007), 124.

52   *Lord, don't you care that my sister:* Luke 10:40–42, NIV.

52   *Laura often complained in her newspaper columns:* Hines, *Laura Ingalls Wilder, Farm Journalist.* At least 10 percent of Laura's *Missouri Ruralist* output of over 170 columns were about feeling overworked.

52 *Also, Laura was a joiner and doer:* John E. Miller, *Laura Ingalls Wilder and Rose Wilder Lane: Authorship, Place, Time, and Culture* (Columbia: University of Missouri Press, 2008), 102.

52 *The harried homemaker complained:* Hines, *Laura Ingalls Wilder, Farm Journalist,* 106–7.

53 *It had been a busy day and I was very tired:* Quoted in Hines, *Laura Ingalls Wilder, Farm Journalist,* 157–58.

55 *she extolled a less traveled way to town:* Hines, *Laura Ingalls Wilder, Farm Journalist,* 244–45.

55 *when, after the effort of climbing:* Quoted in Hines, *Laura Ingalls Wilder, Farm Journalist,* 244–45.

56 *as her grandparents are portrayed as doing:* Laura Ingalls Wilder, *Little House in the Big Woods* (1932; repr., New York: HarperTrophy, 1971), 117–55.

56 *her neighbors in the Ozarks offered:* Stephen W. Hines, ed., *Little House in the Ozarks: The Rediscovered Writings* (Nashville: Thomas Nelson, 1991), 22–23.

56 *She gets eggs in the winter:* Quoted in Hines, *Little House in the Ozarks,* 21.

56 *As much as Laura loved her pa:* Laura Ingalls Wilder, *On the Banks of Plum Creek* (1937; repr., New York: HarperTrophy, 1971), 34–36.

56 *A woman's work is never done:* Quoted in John Bartlett, *Familiar Quotations* (London: Routledge, 1883), 584.

57 *heaped dishes of mashed potatoes:* Laura Ingalls Wilder, *Little Town on the Prairie* (1941; repr., New York: HarperTrophy, 1971), 228.

57 *Later, when all the cleanup was done:* Wilder, *Little Town on the Prairie,* 231–32.

58 *Many years later in a* Ruralist *column:* Hines, *Laura Ingalls Wilder, Farm Journalist,* 267.

58 *Pa remarks . . . that women were an irresistible force:* Wilder, *Little Town on the Prairie,* 55.

59 *Flaring headlines in the papers:* Quoted in Hines, *Laura Ingalls Wilder, Farm Journalist,* 179–81.

60 *Laura quoted a typical Vermont housewife:* Hines, ed., *Little House in the Ozarks,* 195–96.

Chapter 6: Laura and Rose

61 *The pioneers weren't psalm-singers:* Quoted in Stephen W. Hines, *"I Remember Laura"* (Nashville: Thomas Nelson, 1994), 202–3.

62 *Humans were the measure of all things:* William Holtz, *The Ghost in the Little House: A Life of Rose Wilder Lane* (Columbia: University of Missouri Press, 1993), 326–27.

63 *For Mama Bess, getting her own way:* Sallie Ketcham, *Laura Ingalls Wilder: American Writer on the Prairie* (New York and London: Routledge, 2015), 90.

63 *A neighbor once remarked to Laura:* Stephen W. Hines, ed., *Laura Ingalls Wilder, Farm Journalist: Writings from the Ozarks* (Columbia: University of Missouri Press, 2007), 5–6.

63 *it was Laura who chose the very land:* Donald Zochert, *Laura: The Life of Laura Ingalls Wilder* (Chicago: Contemporary Books, 1976), 218.

64 *she is uncomfortable with using the customary word:* Laura Ingalls Wilder, *These Happy Golden Years* (1943; repr., New York: HarperTrophy, 1971), 269–70.

64 *she produced a daughter every bit as strong willed as she:* Holtz, *Ghost in the Little House,* 196–97.

65 *the "lazy, lousy, Lizy Jane":* Laura Ingalls Wilder, *Little Town on the Prairie* (1941; repr., New York: HarperTrophy, 1971), 171, 173.

66 *she made it clear that she did not approve:* Stephen W. Hines, ed., *Little House in the Ozarks: The Rediscovered Writings* (Nashville: Thomas Nelson, 1991), 183–90.

67 *There were old maids when I was a girl:* Hines, ed., *Laura Ingalls Wilder, Farm Journalist,* 149–50.

67 *a writing career at the* San Francisco Bulletin: John E. Miller, *Laura Ingalls Wilder and Rose Wilder Lane: Authorship, Place, Time, and Culture* (Columbia: University of Missouri Press, 2008), 3.

68 *A visit to Rose in 1915:* Laura Ingalls Wilder, *West from Home,* ed. Roger Lea MacBride (New York: HarperTrophy, 1974), xiii, 5, 54.

68 *William Holtz has called the work:* Holtz, *Ghost in the Little House,* 76.

68 *this effort by Rose comes from the* Bulletin *itself:* Rose Wilder Lane, "The City That's Upside Down," Rose Wilder Lane papers, Herbert Hoover Library, West Branch, Iowa. It was published in the *San Francisco Bulletin,* probably in 1915.

69 *homekeeping hearts are happiest:* Hines, ed., *Laura Ingalls Wilder, Farm Journalist,* 7, 70.

70   *at the Fourth of July event:* Wilder, *Little Town on the Prairie,*
     72–75.

70   *Americans won't obey any king on earth:* Wilder, *Little Town
     on the Prairie,* 76.

71   *God is America's king:* Wilder, *Little Town on the Prairie,*
     75.

71   *a rock in a weary land:* Laura Ingalls Wilder, *The Long Winter*
     (1940; repr., New York: HarperTrophy, 1971), 130.

71   *Mary had always been good:* Wilder, *Little Town on the
     Prairie,* 11–13.

73   *It seems to be instinctive:* Quoted in Hines, *Laura Ingalls
     Wilder, Farm Journalist,* 292–93.

73   *the greatness and goodness of God:* Quoted in Hines, *Laura
     Ingalls Wilder, Farm Journalist,* 210.

74   *Mrs. G and I were in a group:* Quoted in Hines, *Laura Ingalls
     Wilder, Farm Journalist,* 170; "The Fool's Prayer" quoted by
     Laura is by Edward Rowland Sill.

75   *Pa assures her that:* Laura Ingalls Wilder, *By the Shores of Silver
     Lake* (1939; repr., New York: HarperTrophy, 1971), 8–14.

75   *Laura continued to have:* Hines, ed., *Little House in the
     Ozarks,* 296.

75   *Here and there one sees a criticism of Christianity:* Quoted in
     Hines, *Laura Ingalls Wilder, Farm Journalist,* 208.

75   *Therefore, Laura insisted that we should:* Quoted in Hines,
     Laura Ingalls Wilder, Farm Journalist, 152–53.

76   *If there were a cry of "stop thief!":* Quoted in Hines, *Laura
     Ingalls Wilder, Farm Journalist,* 152.

76   *Laura reflected on an argument among neighbors:* Quoted in
     Hines, *Laura Ingalls Wilder, Farm Journalist,* 262.

77   *The symbols and even the essentials of religious belief:* Quoted in Hines, *"I Remember Laura,"* 202–3.

78   *I heard a boy swear the other day:* Quoted in Hines, *Laura Ingalls Wilder, Farm Journalist,* 155–56.

79   *Catholic journalist G. K. Chesterton once wrote:* G. K. Chesterton, *Orthodoxy* (New York: Doubleday, 1990), 120.

79   *You have so much tact:* Quoted in Hines, *Laura Ingalls Wilder, Farm Journalist,* 85–86.

80   *when they lived so close together:* Holtz, *Ghost in the Little House,* 227.

Chapter 7: Building the Little House

81   *Just come and visit Rocky Ridge:* Quoted in Stephen W. Hines, ed., *Little House in the Ozarks: The Rediscovered Writings* (Nashville: Thomas Nelson, 1991), 40.

81   *Laura didn't like to hear people testify at prayer meeting:* Laura Ingalls Wilder, *Pioneer Girl: The Annotated Autobiography,* ed. Pamela Smith Hill (Pierre: South Dakota Historical Society Press, 2014), 136.

82   *Rose loved Mama Bess but couldn't get her to take the writing counsel:* William Holtz, *The Ghost in the Little House: A Life of Rose Wilder Lane* (Columbia: University of Missouri Press, 1993), 85–86.

83   *Rose was making several hundred dollars:* Holtz, *Ghost in the Little House,* 150.

84   *Now I have come back to the farm:* Quoted in Irene Lichty Le Count, ed., *Laura Ingalls Wilder: Family, Home and Friends* (Mansfield, MO: self-published, 1980), 19–21.

85	*travel first to Paris and then to Albania:* Holtz, *Ghost in the Little House,* 161–63.

87	*first estimated at a cost of $2,000:* Holtz, *Ghost in the Little House,* 194–96.

88	*This morning was not yet light:* Quoted in Le Count, *Laura Ingalls Wilder,* 15–16.

94	*In the scene in chapter 5:* Laura Ingalls Wilder, *Little House on the Prairie* (1935; repr., New York: HarperTrophy, 1971), 64.

95	*I tend to side with those scholars:* Pamela Smith Hill, *Laura Ingalls Wilder: A Writer's Life* (Pierre: South Dakota State Historical Society Press, 2007), 116–22; John E. Miller, *Laura Ingalls Wilder and Rose Wilder Lane: Authorship, Place, Time, and Culture* (Columbia: University of Missouri Press, 2008), 141–58; and William Anderson, "Laura Ingalls Wilder: Frontier Times Remembered," *American History Illustrated* 19, no. 5 (September 1984): 13, 44–45.

96	*Hill cited a letter Rose wrote to her mother:* Hill, *Laura Ingalls Wilder,* 135–37.

Chapter 8: Songs in the Night

97	*I picked a wild sunflower:* Quoted in Stephen W. Hines, ed., *Little House in the Ozarks: The Rediscovered Writings* (Nashville: Thomas Nelson, 1991), 64.

97	*Humorous tunes such as "The Arkansas Traveler":* Dale Cockrell, ed., *The Happy Land Companion* (Nashville: NDX Press, 2005), 1, 10–13, 29–32.

98	*Hail Columbia, happy land!:* Laura Ingalls Wilder, *By the Shores of Silver Lake* (1939; repr., New York: HarperTrophy, 1971), 154.

98	*future and a hope:* Jeremiah 29:11, NASB.

99 *his father's farm in Spring Valley, Minnesota:* Evelyn Thur-
    man, *The Ingalls—Wilder Homesites* (Bowling Green, KY:
    Kelley Printing Co., 1992), 52–54.

100 *When gloomy clouds across the sky:* John M. Evans, "Jesus
    Holds My Hand," in *Pure Gold for the Sunday School,* ed.
    Robert Lowry and W. Howard Doane (New York: Biglow &
    Main, 1871), 85.

101 *a mysterious way, His wonders to perform:* William Cowper,
    "God Moves in a Mysterious Way," in *The Methodist Hymnal*
    (Nashville: Methodist Publishing House, 1939), 68.

101 *This was thought to be possible and was preached:* Kenneth Scott
    Latourette, *A History of Christianity,* rev. ed., vol. 2, *Reformation
    to the Present* (New York: Harper & Row, 1975), 1163.

102 *Moody admitted:* John Pollock, *Moody* (Chicago: Moody Press,
    1983), 87–91.

103 *Yes! a brighter morn is breaking:* Robert Lowry, "Mountain of
    the Lord," in Lowry and Doane, *Pure Gold,* 52.

104 *"Ma's favorite" hymn:* Andrew Young, "The Happy Land," in
    Cockrell, *Happy Land Companion,* 17.

104 *There is a happy land:* Young, "The Happy Land," in Cockrell,
    Happy Land Companion, 17–18.

105 *Oh, roll the ole chariot along:* "Roll the Ole Chariot Along," in
    Cockrell, *Happy Land Companion,* 37–38. The author of this
    song is anonymous.

106 *Then came a time when reformer Martin Luther:* Robert J.
    Morgan, *Then Sings My Soul* (Nashville: Thomas Nelson,
    2003), 15.

107 *Jesus loves me! this I know:* "Jesus Loves Me," in Lowry and
    Doane, *Pure Gold,* 155.

107   *"Rock of Ages," by Augustus Toplady:* Augustus Toplady, "Rock of Ages," in Lowry and Doane, *Pure Gold,* 155.

109   *When I can read my title clear:* Isaac Watts, "When I Can Read My Title Clear," Hymnary.org, https://hymnary.org/text/when _i_can_read_my_title_clear; see also Laura Ingalls Wilder, *The Long Winter* (1940; repr., New York: HarperTrophy, 1971), 290.

111   *Am I a soldier of the cross:* Isaac Watts, "Am I a Soldier of the Cross?" in *The Methodist Hymnal,* 284.

112   *Shall I be carried to the skies:* Laura Ingalls Wilder, *Little House in the Big Woods* (1932; repr., New York: HarperTrophy, 1971), 97.

112   *the anniversary issue of the* De Smet News *in 1930: De Smet News,* June 6, 1930. Many, many people from Laura's childhood were mentioned.

113   *When tests of character come in later years:* Quoted in Stephen W. Hines, ed., *Laura Ingalls Wilder, Farm Journalist: Writings from the Ozarks* (Columbia: University of Missouri Press, 2007), 291.

115   *Watts wrote hundreds of hymns:* Morgan, *Then Sings My Soul,* 31, 35.

115   *Crosby wrote thousands of hymns:* Robert J. Morgan, *Then Sings My Soul: Book Two* (Nashville: Thomas Nelson, 2004), 121.

115   *The publishers of* Pure Gold *took a shortcut:* Lowry and Doane, *Pure Gold,* 135.

115   *Joyful once again we sing:* Fanny Crosby, "Our Sabbath Home," in Lowry and Doane, *Pure Gold,* 23.

116   *Laura gets rebellious:* Wilder, *Little House in the Big Woods,* 86–96.

116   *Given the books' subject matter:* Dale Cockrell, "Writing the Great American Family Songbook," in *The Ingalls Wilder*

Family Songbook, ed. Dale Cockrell (Middleton, WI: A-R Editions, 2011), xviii–xix.

117 *We are going forth with our staff in hand:* Fanny Crosby, "The Good Old Way," in Lowry and Doane, *Pure Gold,* 18.

117 *I realize that all my life:* Hines, *Little House in the Ozarks,* 64.

118 *Rob and Ella Boast arrive:* Wilder, *By the Shores of Silver Lake,* 182–83.

118 *Merry, merry Christmas everywhere:* Mrs. T. J. Cook, "Merry, Merry Christmas!" in Lowry and Doane, *Pure Gold,* 150; see also Wilder, *By the Shores of Silver Lake,* 187.

119 *two additional songs the Ingallses associated with Christmas:* Wilder, *By the Shores of Silver Lake,* 181–82.

119 *"Mountain of the Lord":* Lowry and Doane, *Pure Gold,* 52.

119 *"Gentle Words and Loving Smiles":* Lowry and Doane, *Pure Gold,* 139.

120 *It is not much the world can give:* Wilder, *By the Shores of Silver Lake,* 182.

121 *He and Ma and Mary spent their last years:* De Smet News, June 6, 1930.

121 *As a citizen he was held in high esteem:* "A Pioneer Gone," *De Smet News,* June 12, 1902, http://beyondlittlehouse.com/2011/06/09/anniversary-of-the-death-of-charles-pa-ingalls-june-8/.

122 *There's a land that is fairer than day:* Sanford Fillmore Bennett, "Sweet By and By," in Cockrell, *Happy Land Companion,* 39–40.

Chapter 9: The Church Potluck

125 *Thinking of pies and poems:* Quoted in Stephen W. Hines, ed., *Laura Ingalls Wilder, Farm Journalist: Writings from*

the *Ozarks* (Columbia: University of Missouri Press, 2007), 307.

126   *The* Cream City Cook Book *was published in 1914:* All the recipes in this chapter come from Aid Society Congregational Church, comp., *Cream City Cook Book* (De Smet, SD; reprinted by the *De Smet News* in 1979 for the Laura Ingalls Wilder Memorial Society, 1904–14).

127   *They always lived on their claim:* Laura Ingalls Wilder, *The Long Winter* (1940; repr., New York: HarperTrophy, 1971), 325.

Chapter 10: What Laura Means to Us

155   *Mankind is not following a blind trail:* Quoted in Stephen W. Hines, ed., *Laura Ingalls Wilder, Farm Journalist: Writings from the Ozarks* (Columbia: University of Missouri Press, 2007), 292–93.

156   *real things haven't changed:* Laura Ingalls Wilder, *The Selected Letters of Laura Ingalls Wilder,* ed. William Anderson (New York: HarperCollins, 2016), 284.

156   *I noted that he used the striking phrase:* Dale Cockrell, "Writing the Great American Family Songbook," in *The Ingalls Wilder Family Songbook,* ed. Dale Cockrell, (Middleton, WI: A-R Editions, 2011), xix.

157   *After being taunted by Mary:* Stephen W. Hines, ed., *Little House in the Ozarks: The Rediscovered Writings* (Nashville: Thomas Nelson, 1991), 297–98.

158   *Her sister Carrie remarked:* Hines, *Little House in the Ozarks,* 91.

158   *She wrote about receiving a letter:* Hines, *Little House in the Ozarks,* 89.

158   *When Laura and Almanzo were starting:* Hines, *Little House in the Ozarks,* 230.

159   *Mr. Skelton was a good borrower:* Quoted in Hines, *Little House in the Ozarks,* 230.

160   *There is no elation:* Quoted in Hines, *Little House in the Ozarks,* 239.

Appendix 1: Remembering the De Smet of Old

163   *Pa Ingalls was credited as being the first settler:* "Ingalls Was First Resident De Smet: Family of R. R. Timekeeper Lived at Silver Lake in 1879; Moved to Town," *De Smet News,* June 6, 1930.

163   *got lost three times:* Donald Zochert, *Laura: The Life of Laura Ingalls Wilder* (Chicago: Contemporary Books, 1976), 236.

163   *De Smet celebration was the highlight:* Irene Lichty Le Count, ed., *Laura Ingalls Wilder: Family, Home and Friends* (Mansfield, MO: self-published, 1980), 50–53.

163   *Eliza Jane Wilder . . . had also given up her claim:* William Holtz, *The Ghost in the Little House: A Life of Rose Wilder Lane* (Columbia: University of Missouri Press, 1993), 41.

164   *The little town we used to know:* Quoted in Le Count, *Laura Ingalls Wilder,* 52.

165   *had also largely populated the first church:* "De Smet's Pioneer Church Is Celebrating Fiftieth Anniversary This Year, Too," *De Smet News,* June 6, 1930.

165   *Ever I see them in my mental vision:* Quoted in Stephen W. Hines, *"I Remember Laura"* (Nashville: Thomas Nelson, 1994), 17; Laura's poem originally appeared in the *De Smet News,* June 20, 1930.

166   *Ingalls Was First Resident De Smet:* "Ingalls Was First Resident De Smet," *De Smet News.*

170   *De Smet's Pioneer Church:* "De Smet's Pioneer Church," *De Smet News.*

172   *CHURCHES:* Aubrey Sherwood, *Beginnings of De Smet* (De Smet, SD: Aubrey Sherwood, 1979), 11.

Appendix 2: An Interview with Laura's Friend Neta Seal

175   *Perhaps Laura's best friend:* Stephen W. Hines, *"I Remember Laura"* (Nashville: Thomas Nelson, 1994), 105.

175   *When I say retirement with regard to Laura:* William Holtz, *The Ghost in the Little House: A Life of Rose Wilder Lane* (Columbia: University of Missouri Press, 1993), 292–93.

176   *How we met the Wilders is sort of a long story:* From an interview from the early 1990s and stored on CD. The printed interview comes from Hines, *"I Remember Laura,"* 106–13.

178   *Waltz me around, O Willy:* Neta sang this from memory and may have conflated two songs. I wasn't able to identify this version.

178   *She drives a Cadillac:* This song seems to derive, in part, from a folk tune "My Gal's a Corker," which in the original lyrics has nothing to do with either Fords or Cadillacs.

179   *Carrie had married a widowed miner:* John E. Miller, *Becoming Laura Ingalls Wilder: The Woman Behind the Legend* (Columbia: University of Missouri Press, 1998), 226.

181   *Almanzo grew apples:* Stephen W. Hines, ed., *Laura Ingalls Wilder, Farm Journalist: Writings from the Ozarks* (Columbia: University of Missouri Press, 2007), 20–22.

182   *Helen Burkhiser did a book on me:* That book or booklet was Helen Burkhiser, *Neta, Laura's Friend* (privately printed, 1989).

Bibliography

Aid Society Congregational Church, comp. *Cream City Cook Book.*
De Smet, SD. Reprinted by the *De Smet News* in 1979 for the
Laura Ingalls Wilder Memorial Society, 1904–14.

Anderson, William. "A Journey Through the Land of 'Little Houses.'"
American History Illustrated 19, no. 5 (September 1984): 14–19.

———. *Laura Ingalls Wilder: A Biography.* New York: Harper-
Collins, 1992.

——— "Laura Ingalls Wilder and Rose Wilder Lane: The Continuing Collaboration." *South Dakota History* 16 (Summer 1986):
89–143.

———. "Laura Ingalls Wilder: Frontier Times Remembered."
American History Illustrated 19, no. 5 (September 1984): 8–13,
44–45.

———. "The Literary Apprenticeship of Laura Ingalls Wilder."
South Dakota History 13 (Winter 1983): 285–331.

———, ed. *A Little House Reader.* New York: HarperCollins,
1998.

———, ed. *A Little House Sampler: Laura Ingalls Wilder and Rose
Wilder Lane.* Lincoln: University of Nebraska Press, 1988.

Bartlett, John. *Familiar Quotations.* London: Routledge, 1883.

Bunyan, John. *The Pilgrim's Progress.* New York: New American
Library of World Literature, 1964.

Burkhiser, Helen. *Neta, Laura's Friend.* Privately printed, 1989.

Chesterton, G. K. *Orthodoxy.* New York: Doubleday, 1990.

Cockrell, Dale, ed. *The Happy Land Companion*. Nashville: NDX Press, 2005.

———, ed. *The Ingalls Wilder Family Songbook*. Middleton, WI: A-R Editions, 2011.

Dathe, Mary Jo. *Spring Valley: The Laura Ingalls Wilder Connection*. Spring Valley, MN: Spring Valley Tribune, 1990.

"De Smet's Pioneer Church Is Celebrating Fiftieth Anniversary This Year, Too." *De Smet News*. June 6, 1930.

Fellman, Anita Clair. *Little House, Long Shadow: Laura Ingalls Wilder's Impact on American Culture*. Columbia: University of Missouri Press, 2008.

Harding, Neva. *I Recall Pioneer Days in South Dakota*. Brookings, SD: The Woman's Club and The Saturday Literary Club, 1972.

Hawkins, Barb, and George Hawkins. *Laura Ingalls Wilder and the Family Journey*. Applegate, MI: Barbara Hawkins Little House Site Tours, 2013.

Hill, Pamela Smith. *Laura Ingalls Wilder: A Writer's Life*. Pierre: South Dakota Historical Society Press, 2007.

Hines, Stephen W. *"I Remember Laura."* Nashville: Thomas Nelson, 1994.

———, ed. *Laura Ingalls Wilder, Farm Journalist: Writings from the Ozarks*. Columbia: University of Missouri Press, 2007.

———, ed. *Little House in the Ozarks: The Rediscovered Writings*. Nashville: Thomas Nelson, 1991.

———, ed. *Saving Graces: The Inspirational Writings of Laura Ingalls Wilder*. Nashville: Broadman & Holman, 1997.

Holtz, William. *The Ghost in the Little House: A Life of Rose Wilder Lane*. Columbia: University of Missouri Press, 1993.

"Ingalls Was First Resident De Smet: Family of R. R. Timekeeper Lived at Silver Lake in 1879; Moved to Town." *De Smet News.* June 6, 1930.

Ketcham, Sallie. *Laura Ingalls Wilder: American Writer on the Prairie.* New York: Routledge, 2015.

Korda, Michael. *Making the List.* New York: Barnes & Noble Books, 2001.

Lane, Rose Wilder. "The City That's Upside Down." Rose Wilder Lane papers, Herbert Hoover Library, West Branch, Iowa. Published in the *San Francisco Bulletin,* probably in 1915.

————. *Free Land.* Reprint, Lincoln, NE: Bison Books, 1984.

————. *Let the Hurricane Roar.* Reprint, New York: HarperTrophy, 1985.

————. *Old Home Town.* Reprint, Lincoln, NE: Bison Books, 1985.

Latourette, Kenneth Scott. *A History of Christianity.* Rev. ed. Vol. 2, *Reformation to the Present.* New York: Harper & Row, 1975.

Le Count, Irene Lichty, ed. *Laura Ingalls Wilder: Family, Home and Friends.* Mansfield, MO: self-published, 1980.

Lichty, Irene V. *The Ingalls Family from Plum Creek to Walnut Grove via Burr Oak, Iowa.* Mansfield, MO: self-published, 1970.

Lowry, Robert, and W. Howard Doane, eds. *Pure Gold for the Sunday School.* New York: Biglow & Main, 1871.

McClure, Wendy. *The Wilder Life: My Adventures in the Lost World of Little House on the Prairie.* New York: Riverhead Books, 2011.

The Methodist Hymnal. Nashville: Methodist Publishing House, 1939.

Michener, James A. *The World Is My Home.* New York: Random House, 1991.

Miller, John E. *Becoming Laura Ingalls Wilder: The Woman Behind the Legend.* Columbia: University of Missouri Press, 1998.

———. *Laura Ingalls Wilder and Rose Wilder Lane: Authorship, Place, Time, and Culture.* Columbia: University of Missouri Press, 2008.

Moore, Rosa Ann. "Laura Ingalls Wilder's Orange Notebooks and the Art of the Little House Books." *Children's Literature* 4 (1975): 105–19.

———. "The Little House Books: Rose-Colored Classics." *Children's Literature* 7 (1978): 7–16.

Morgan, Robert J. *Then Sings My Soul.* Nashville: Thomas Nelson, 2003.

———. *Then Sings My Soul: Book Two.* Nashville: Thomas Nelson, 2004.

The Pa's Fiddle Project: Featuring the Music of the Little House Books. Laura Ingalls Wilder.com. Pa's Fiddle Recordings, LLC, 2015. www.laura-ingalls-wilder.com/index.htm.

"A Pioneer Gone." *De Smet News,* June 12, 1902. http://beyond littlehouse.com/2011/06/09/anniversary-of-the-death-of-charles -pa-ingalls-june-8/.

Riders in the Sky. "The Arkansas Traveler." *The Arkansas Traveler: Music from Little House on the Prairie.* Produced by Butch Baldassari and Dale Cockrell. Cackle & Splash Music, 2006.

Rölvaag, Ole E. *Giants in the Earth.* New York: Harper & Brothers, 1927.

Rowen, Clyde A., ed. *History and Families, Wright County, Missouri.* Paducah, KY: Turner Publishing, 1993.

Sherwood, Aubrey. *Beginnings of De Smet.* De Smet, SD: Aubrey Sherwood, 1979.

Simonson, Harold P. *Beyond the Frontier: Writers, Western Regionalism and a Sense of Place.* Fort Worth: Texas Christian University Press, 1989.

Stone, Tanya Lee. *Laura Ingalls Wilder.* New York: DK Publishing, 2009.

Thurman, Evelyn. *The Ingalls—Wilder Homesites.* Bowling Green, KY: Kelley Printing Co., 1992.

Vogt, Scott. "Buffalograss: Five Keys to a Successful Planting." Dyck Arboretum of the Plains. June 3, 2015. http://dyckarboretum.org /buffalograss-five-keys-successful-planting/.

Wilder, Laura Ingalls. *By the Shores of Silver Lake.* New York: HarperTrophy, 1971. First published 1939.

———. *Farmer Boy.* New York: HarperTrophy, 1971. First published 1933.

———. *The First Four Years.* New York: HarperTrophy, 1971.

———. *Little House in the Big Woods.* New York: HarperTrophy, 1971. First published 1932.

———. *Little House on the Prairie.* New York: HarperTrophy, 1971. First published 1935.

———. *A Little House Traveler.* New York: HarperCollins, 2006.

———. *Little Town on the Prairie.* New York: HarperTrophy, 1971. First published 1941.

———. *The Long Winter.* New York: HarperTrophy, 1971. First published 1940.

———. "Notes from the Real Little House on the Prairie." Edited by Roger Lea MacBride. *Saturday Evening Post* (September 1978): 56–57, 104–5.

———. *On the Banks of Plum Creek.* New York: HarperTrophy, 1971. First published 1937.

———. *On the Way Home.* New York: HarperTrophy, 1976. First published 1962.

———. *Pioneer Girl: The Annotated Autobiography.* Edited by Pamela Smith Hill. Pierre: South Dakota Historical Society Press, 2014.

———. *The Selected Letters of Laura Ingalls Wilder.* Edited by William Anderson. New York: HarperCollins, 2016.

———. *These Happy Golden Years.* New York: HarperTrophy, 1971. First published 1943.

———. *West from Home.* Edited by Roger Lea MacBride. New York: HarperTrophy, 1974.

Williams, Oscar. *A Pocket Book of Modern Verse.* New York: Washington Square Press, 1960.

Zochert, Donald. *Laura: The Life of Laura Ingalls Wilder.* Chicago: Contemporary Books, 1976.

Index